Keefer: The People's Choice

Leslie A Wootten

Keith Dillon

Keefer

The People's Choice

Leslie A. Wootten

Copyright © 2007 Leslie A. Wootten
All rights reserved

ISBN–13–978-0-9795885-2-5 (pbk.)
ISBN–10–0-9795885-2-9

Written by Leslie A. Wootten
Casa Grande, Arizona
www.lesliewootten.net

Book design, photo restoration and layout by Marion Johnson
THE MEMORY WORKS, LLC
Sedona, Arizona
www.memoryworkspublishing.com

The text of this book was set in Garamond 3 and Windsor EF-Light.

CONTENTS

Forward

When the two previous generations of one's family have been life-long participants in the same endeavor, you might expect the third generation to follow in their footsteps and be totally engrossed in the same venture. Either that, or shun the activity altogether.

In Leslie Wootten's case, it's definitely the former—which can be attested to by anyone who's read any of her writings about Greyhound racing. Her passion for the Greyhound game is evident in the opening sentences of every story she writes.

I suspect that her enthusiasm comes largely from a sense of pride in her own family, which has been immersed in the sport going back to the late 1800s. There's definitely an emotional connection there—between the Greyhound breed and Leslie (she now has two retired Greyhounds as pets)—and it's a connection that she ardently embraces. Her devoted readers are privileged that she's chosen to share that connection with them.

Leslie is a Greyhound historian—a fact no doubt spawned by the Wootten family's involvement with the breed when they coursed their hounds over the open prairies and farm fields of the West and Midwest in a bygone era. This was many years before the world's fastest canines ever set foot on an oval track in pursuit of an artificial lure. In a way, the story of Greyhound racing is the story of Leslie's own family. How, then, could she possibly *not* carry on a lifelong love affair with the sport? How could she not be enraptured with this thrilling game—this integral part of our own personal history?

Fortunately for us, Leslie is also a gifted storyteller. For years, her human-interest feature articles have graced the pages of the industry's major, national magazine, *The Greyhound Review*, along with other publications. There have been few other Greyhound writers who've approached the colorful, personal stories of those in the Greyhound game with as much sensitivity and enthusiasm. Leslie does more than simply tell a story. In a way, she lives it herself. Moreover, she let's you—the reader—live it, too.

And that's exactly how Leslie has approached the legend of the great Keefer. For those of us in the sport who were already familiar with the stories of the super champ and the people who surrounded him—Keith Dillon, Jim Schulthess, etc.—you'll find this text a tough one to put down once you get started. Even if you are unfamiliar with these personalities, or have never heard of Keefer, I'm confident you'll find the story captivating and entertaining. Why? Because it offers an intriguing glimpse into the amazing sport of Greyhound racing and the awesome breed that makes it all happen. And, because it's a fascinating character study of the lives of just a few of the thousands of incredibly unique people who are and have been a key part of the Greyhound racing scene.

It's a story that Leslie knows—and has lived. It's a story that only someone with her background, insight and talent can properly tell.

Gary Guccione
Exec. Dir, National Greyhound Assn.

Preface

The 1980s were memorable for the speed and innovation of their technological advances, particularly in communication. The first IBM personal computers became available, boasting 64 kilobytes of memory and the hefty price of $2665. After 25,000 sold the first year, millions more flew off the shelves. Cellular phones entered the realm of consumer possibility to the financial tune of $3,000 plus $150 monthly service fees. Megabit memory chips were introduced, and shiny Apple Macintoshes became crisp new favorites. So prevalent and dominant were "thinking machines" that Time's 1982 "man of the year" was a computer.

In the midst of all the technological progress, a red-fawn Greyhound named Keefer entered the world on January 16, 1984. He proceeded to do what Greyhounds had done for centuries—race to beat the clock, the wind, competition, self. During a time when man-made computers leap-frogged into obsolescence soon after assemblage, Keefer represented an aerodynamic wonder of natural perfection, a blend of sublime form and function that defied the need for alteration.

With nothing but a silk racing blanket on his back, Keefer performed—and prevailed—even when he lost according to a *Wall Street Journal* article about him. Never before or since has a racing Greyhound graced the front page of the world's foremost business periodical. In a decade when supply-side economics, corporate raiders, dress for success, and power lunch were key terms in the popular lexicon, the streamlined canine nudged into the limelight, attracting novices as well as racing regulars into his sphere. At a time when "where's the beef?" and "read my lips" were confrontational catch phrases, Keefer had the power to unite, bringing people together in one place, for one purpose—to see a Greyhound they adored as their own. Such a feat was all the more impressive because the charismatic charmer came along at a time when Greyhound racing across the country teetered on the brink of decline due to state lotteries, Indian gaming, and other venues that competed for patrons and their entertainment dollars.

In the 20 years since Keefer's last race, there have been other Greyhounds to rival—and in some cases, surpass—Keefer's racetrack accomplishments. Even so, none have drawn the crowds that he attracted, just as none have "touched" so many lives in so many ways. True, he was the right Greyhound at the right time in the right place, but "right" only goes so far. Beyond the boost, there has to be something solid and sure, something that manages to elude easy definition while leaving no hint of doubt. That would be Keefer, whose story began on a wintry day in Olathe, Kansas.

PART ONE

CHAPTER ONE

"This is the one, Doc.
This is the one."
—Keith Dillon

Keith Dillon and My Judy, winner's circle, Tampa, 1941.

Keith Dillon and the "miracle litter," 1950s.

"This is the One, Doc."

The day of Keefer's birth dawned freezing cold on the Keith Dillon farm in Olathe, Kansas. Dillon stamped snow off his boots before entering the heated kennel where his Greyhounds slept. A clicking key had the effect of a rattling alarm clock. That slight sound knocked dreams loose, and almost instantly, the kennel was awash in barked greetings, all Greyhounds watchful, attention focused on the door.

Dillon's eyes swept through the kennel, mentally taking inventory, making sure his charges were all alert. Granddaddy Downing and his sons, Perceive and Understood, formed a brindle trio of muscled power as they stretched in separate pens. The broods Abella, Economy, and Position posed like ballerinas, ready to spring out of their crates into action. Position's milk had come in, Dillon noticed, and her stomach bulged where it typically arched. The calendar said it was time and so did her body. For Position, there would be no settling into a whelping box to birth naturally. Instead, she would ride with Dillon to the vet's office for a Caesarean. It was a trip the two of them had taken together before. Position didn't mind driving hard to the finish line on the racetrack, but when it came to birthing pups, she couldn't manage the final push without surgical help.

When he turned the dogs into their long-run pens, Dillon watched as they leap-frogged through the snow, their paws spending more time in the air than on the ivory fluff. Their short-hair coats and slight body fat invited cold to sink like ice chips through their skin. Such cold meant there would be no catch-me-if-you-can teases or playful romps, just quick elimination and a scurry back into the kennel's warmth. With thick white flurry carpeting the fields, there would be no sprint work-outs, no whirlygig or jack-a-lure chases. If Position hadn't required the vet, there might have been a round of canine teeth cleaning or toenail clipping, but even that was out now. Position pawed the shredded paper in her box. She was ready.

At the vet's office, Position tugged at her leash, as if to say, "Let's get this over with." Dr. Knappenberger was ready with the I.V. His staff had the surgical room prepped. When the needle slid into a vein in Position's right foreleg, she didn't flinch. Such stoicism combined with rich, ample blood made her, and most Greyhounds, dream donors. Dr. Knappenberger kept a couple of them at his clinic for that very reason. If a blood transfusion was required, his Greyhounds provided a ready supply.

As Dr. Knappenberger lifted pups out of Position's womb, he handed them to Dillon to clean up. It was a task the Greyhound racing veteran knew well. Scrape the filmy birth sack off the nose, assure there was breathing, rub the body dry, snip the stringy umblilical cord, daub with iodine. After 46 years around Greyhounds, Dillon had observed hundreds of pups. Most of the time, they looked like what they were: pudgy furballs that would—with luck and proper training—grow into sleek racing creatures. Dillon knew it was impossible to predict a newborn's future. A pup was just a pup. That day, Dillon's pragmatic view shifted when Dr. Knappenberger lifted the pup that would be Keefer into the world. Dillon cradled the wiggling form in his hands. "This is the one, Doc," he remarked with all the confidence in the world. "This is the one."

Dillon liked the pup's black nose and red-fawn color, he was impressed by his size—weighty even at birth—and the fact that he physically resembled the legendary Traffic Officer, a champion of the 1920s and 1930s. But, it went beyond what could be observed. Dillon embraced the intangible, a realm he typically ignored. Until Keefer, that is, when the 69-year-old Dillon allowed a gut-feeling to supersede reason, and the energy vibrating in his hands to send ripples of certainty to his brain. "This is the one, Doc," he repeated to confirm what he intuitively knew to be fact.

If someone had challenged the remark with a doubting, "You don't know that," Dillon could very easily have replied, "Oh yes, I do." It would not be the first or last time he was infused with overwhelming confidence that others questioned.

Born in Cedar, Kansas, on June 6, 1915, Dillon grew up during the "Roaring Twenties" and the Great Depression of the 1930s. Through good times and bad, he managed to stay focused, graduating from high school in 1932 and going on to earn a degree from Grand Island, Nebraska's Business College in 1935. Despite lean years that hobbled the entire country, a determined young Dillon found paying jobs as meat cutter, store clerk, and construction laborer. He didn't mind hard work and long hours for meager pay, but when a construction supervisor rubbed him the wrong way, 23-year-old Dillon bristled and quit, returning home to Cedar, unemployed and unsure of what was next.

Call it chance or call it fate, but an opportunity with Greyhounds unexpectedly surfaced when out-of-work Dillon needed it most. Cedar's town grocer, J.A. "Prof"

Anderson—future Greyhound Hall of Fame pioneer— asked the young man if he wanted to ready a couple of pups for the 1938 National Fall Sapling. The offer brought no security in the form of a steady paycheck and no possibility of promotion in a corporate chain of command. In Dillon's eyes, though, it brought something even better— the prospect of winning $750, more than half-a-year's wages, for six weeks of being outdoors every day with a couple of pups. It would be a challenge, of course, to get the Greyhounds to their peak performance, but Dillon was ready to try.

"Yes," the 23-year-old said with affirmative conviction. Ever honest, he told Prof that he didn't know anything about Greyhounds, but he could learn. "You tell me what to do and I'll do it," he said, with the resolve that would prove to be his lifelong trademark.

That resolve saw Dillon—and the pups he conditioned—through six steady weeks of focused preparation. Each day, he walked the Greyhounds to the edge of town, then jogged them on the lead for four miles out and four miles back. Every other day, he added sprints. As the Nationals approached, Dillon's confidence swelled. He was so sure of a win that he went on a buying spree for new clothes prior to the meet. When Prof asked why he wasted good money that way, Dillon replied he wanted to look nice when he accepted the Sapling trophy. There was no irony or arrogance in his words, just belief and self-assurance. When Prof walked away shaking his head, Dillon wondered what in the world was wrong with the man.

Dillon's confidence didn't flag one iota when he discovered that over 270 dogs were entered in the Sapling stake. Triumph meant winning nine rounds, with three rounds on the last day. The victor was Dillon-trained Samco. Years later, Dillon made it sound easy to come out on top in the midst of the country's most talented Greyhounds competing against each other under arduous conditions. The win wasn't easy, of course, but the process leading to the meet might have felt easy because it suited Dillon's independent nature so completely.

Upon returning home with his share of the win, Dillon ordered a cup of coffee in Cedar's cafe, plopping down a hundred dollar bill. When people looked incredulous and queried, "Where in the world did you get that?" Dillon proudly replied, "I'm in the dog business."

Indeed he was. Although he'd had the fine taste of success and was definitely committed, he wanted to know more about Greyhounds chasing a mechanical lure around the track. The winter following the Nationals, he went to Tampa, Florida, and hired on with Zene Freeman. His job was primarily cooling out dogs after they raced, but he was an astute observer who also watched, listened and absorbed as much as he could in the racetrack environment. One bit of information that Dillon rejected was Freeman's advice on careers. "Now, Keith, let me tell you something," the fine old gentleman began. "You've got an education and you're a good looking boy. Don't get into this dog business." As well-intentioned as the caution was, Dillon could not be persuaded to veer off the path he'd set for himself. In a 1983 article by Gary Guccione that appeared in *The Greyhound Review*, Dillon remarked that of his $7 a week salary, he spent $2.50 for board, $2.50 for food, and had $2 left for a wager ticket. He didn't need more than that because he let nothing distract him from his single-minded focus. "I could look at every dog that set foot on the track and tell you exactly who they were just by looking at them," he told Guccione.

Dillon was definitely a quick study. Following the winter meet with Freeman, he spent a summer working for Glen Garverick earning $15 a week. After that, Dillon felt ready to set out on his own. In the fall of 1939, he returned to Kansas, leased dogs, borrowed a hauling trailer and $59 on his life insurance, then headed south to Florida for the upcoming Tampa meet. With the same confidence he'd had about winning the Sapling stake, he expected to secure a booking at Tampa just like that. When he got his Greyhounds settled into the kennel compound, he walked over to the track's restaurant to get a bite to eat. On his way, he ran into General Manager Eddie Rouleau who asked what his plans were for the dogs. "I'm going to race them here," Dillon replied as if to say, "What else?" To Rouleau's, "You need a booking and you don't have one," Dillon said, "Well, give me one then." When Rouleau blurted, "Keith, there's no way you can make it," the young man did not flinch. He knew he could. "I borrowed on my life insurance to get here," he said with assurance. "I bought my meat on time." In Dillon's mind, everything was in place for a winning season of racing his dogs. Rouleau walked away shaking his head as Anderson had done before the Nationals. Dillon refused to buy into anyone's doubt. He pressed on with a "You just try me" attitude and he got his booking. Before the meet was over, he proved there was mettle behind his words. With typical understatement, he chuckled about that first venture, and said, "I didn't do too bad." Following what he called a "fair" summer of racing in Memphis, Dillon returned to Tampa the next winter and rocketed up in the kennel standings.

My Judy, a 1939 female out of Judy Squeers by My Bugger, led Dillon into the winner's circle for the Tampa Juvenile Stakes of 1941. It was the young man's first stakes triumph. The presentation photo reveals just how serious Dillon was even in the glow of victory. Grasping the massive trophy, he looked into the camera's eye, square-jawed, intense, no hint of a smile. It was a landmark moment calling for celebration, but the photo reveals no sign that partying was on Dillon's mind.

According to Dillon, My Judy was a dog who liked to pace—and tease. Preferring the front early on, she'd have a two-to-four length lead. As she came around the last turn, she'd slack off heading for the wire. You'd think for a moment she was going to get beat, but she'd keep her nose ahead and win by the tiniest fraction. In 1941, she continued strutting her stuff by winning 9 out of 11 starts at Taunton in Massachusetts. Besides being a crafty champion, though, My Judy had a feisty streak that eventually got her in trouble she couldn't tease her way out of. She won all her races except her last when she got ruled off for interference. The pert brindle went on to become a quality dam, producing two of America's great brood females, My Handy and Handy Judy.

While My Judy and Dillon's other Greyhounds were winning races, the U.S. was gearing up to enter World War II. In fact, after Japan bombed Pearl Harbor on December 7, 1941, Dillon knew it was just a matter of time before he was drafted. No draft notice came, however, and he got through a summer of racing at Taunton followed by another season at Tampa. As June of 1942 approached, the war heated up in Europe and Asia. Dillon went to his draft board in Kansas and asked if he had time for a 50-day meet at Taunton where he had secured a booking. He told the board that if he was going to be drafted right away, he wanted to sell the dogs and save traveling to Massachusetts. Since the board's reply was, "Sure, you've got time. Go on," that's what he did. The advice proved faulty when a draft notice arrived during schooling before the meet even began. Dillon had to scramble to get his affairs in order, and this meant selling quality Greyhounds at bargain basement prices.

Around the time he quizzed the draft board in 1942, he ventured to a dance sponsored by the Areon Defense Plant near Kansas City. Young women working in war-related jobs attended these events to cheer, support, and entertain men who would soon be heading overseas. Dances generally weren't high on Dillon's list of things to do. He couldn't say why he attended that particular night, but it was lucky that he did because love was about to strike. "I looked across the room, and there was the prettiest girl I'd ever seen," Dillon remarked. "I went over and we got to visiting." It might have been luck that sent Dillon to the dance that night, pure chance that he happened to glance across the room when he did. Soon afterwards, though, chance and luck fell by the wayside. Dillon knew with certainty that Viv, as he called her, was the woman for him. Determination took over to make her his wife. After a six-week courtship, Dillon and Viv began a marriage that would thrive through the peaks and valleys that life assures.

Luckily, Keith and Viv Dillon's six-week courtship established a solid foundation of commitment and strength they could both count on when apart. Shortly after their wedding, the young groom's World War II army duty took him to the other side of the earth. Hand-scrawled letters had to serve as the only means of communication in a time when mail delivery was spotty for soldiers overseas. In the South Pacific where Dillon was based, his position as First Sergeant kept him busy supervising 250 men. Viv busied herself by working full-time in a job that supported the war effort.

As 1946 unfolded, the couple resumed building a life together. With the War over, Vivian quit her job and Dillon put away his army clothes, duty to his country fulfilled. Back in civilian mode, the couple chose to plunge back into traveling the Greyhound racing circuit. After a brief welcome home in Kansas, they hastily packed their bags and headed to Florida. Dillon didn't have any dogs, but he went to the Tampa racetrack prepared to talk his way into a booking if necessary. When General Manager Eddie Rouleau saw him, he didn't shake his head like he had the first time. He sported no worried frown or admonition that Dillon couldn't make it. Instead, he immediately proclaimed, "You're booked. Now, get yourself some dogs."

Get dogs is exactly what Dillon did in a hurry. He called home and had six Greyhounds sent down from Kansas. He also took over the management of four racers that Stubb Life had running at the Tampa track. Life wanted to go home and all he asked of Dillon was that at the end of the meet, he return the dogs and his trailer to him in Nebraska. It was a deal.

The following summer, Dillon said yes to Babe Diamond's request to run his dogs at Revere in Massachusetts. Although he would lease Diamond's kennel in the fall of 1948, Dillon itched to have his own dogs again. In between meets, he and Viv went on a buying spree using their War Bond savings of several thousand dollars. Traveling through Kansas, the pair purchased a pup here, a pup there. Out of the 13 pups they randomly purchased, 12 went to top of the line, Grade A. When Dillon and Diamond parted ways, Dillon secured a booking at Biscayne and Flagler, winning the Puppy Stakes as well as the Flagler Futurity. He spent a summer racing at Denver where his kennel kicked off a winning season by capturing the Inaugural.

In the early 1950s, Dillon unveiled what became known as the "Miracle Litter" out of K.C. Byers and My Handy. Dillon had the magic touch in raising and training this litter because all eight became Grade A racers. In his 1983 *Greyhound Review* article, Guccione noted that the miracle pups were so "talented and evenly matched that Flagler staged an eight-dog race featuring all the dogs in the litter."

What were Dillon's secrets? Actually, the biggest secret was that he had no secrets. He had no particular mentors, either, though he learned from Prof Anderson to feed his dogs extremely well. Dillon noted that Prof cooked oatmeal for his Greyhounds daily and mixed in meat scraps he bought for 2 cents a pound. The dogs loved the mixture, and they thrived on it. Besides feeding his dogs well, what Dillon relied on as much as anything was a prompt and regular routine the dogs could depend on. His schedule of rising at 5:30 every morning to begin chores was one he followed faithfully throughout his career, regardless of the day or season. When he reduced his workload in later years, he didn't alter his schedule, which continued to suit him and his Greyhounds well.

One of Dillon's greatest "tools" in his chosen trade was a simple virtue that has been bandied about in every walk of life for thousands of years: patience. Patience didn't mean waiting until his Greyhounds were 12 months of age before he began working with them. In fact, at 3 months he'd begin training pups to walk on a lead and to stand calmly on the grooming bench as he got them used to rub-downs, nail clippings, teeth exams and cleanings. He also got them used to going out to a large field for exercise. At 10 months, he "schooled" them in individual crates. When it was time to begin chase training at 11-12 months, the pups were well-mannered and ready to pay attention to the job at hand.

Patience was essential—crucial—in the kind of train-ing that Dillon used exclusively from 1972 forward. That was the year he perfected his "Jack-a-Lure" invention, a device that basically replaced the use of live lures in train-ing. It was, of course, easier in some ways to use live jackrabbits because Greyhounds—all dogs really—are prey animals with the instinct to track and catch live creatures for survival. Like Labrador Retrievers and other hunting dogs, Greyhounds were bred over centuries to catch and retrieve prey, returning it to their humans to put food on the table. Although Dillon grew up around coursing where live prey was central to the chase, he was not a die-hard like some old-timers who believed Greyhounds had to have the taste of blood to race at their best. Some of the pioneers were convinced that the taste of blood in training gave their dogs the guts to power through traffic jams at the first turn and beyond in pursuit of the mechanical lure at the track. Dillon instinctively knew it wasn't so, and he proved it with his innovative design.

The Jack-a-Lure was inspired by a coonskin cap Dillon saw while vacationing in Denver. It caught his eye because the cap was the exact color of a jackrabbit. Back home, he experimented by stuffing the cap with paper and a predator call that squawked when the cap dragged on the ground. Before long, Dillon had the training device ready to test on his pups. He wasn't surprised that it worked every bit as well as jackrabbits without the bloody mess. True, it took a little longer—and more patience on his part—to get the pups used to chasing the dummy device, but once they caught on, they chased it with assertive vigor. That vigor transferred to subsequent whirlygig training and, ultimately, the racetrack. The very first litter Dillon trained on his invention ran 1-2 in the toughest race at Southland, one of the most competitive tracks in the nation, then went on to claim first in the All-American Derby at Taunton in Massachusetts, another crème de la crème race at a premiere track. These wins and the many that followed convinced Dillon that his Jack-a-Lure was the real deal, a viable, practical, and ultimately essential, alternative.

Essential because Dillon had foreseen that live jackrabbit use was headed for obsolescence. In the fall of 1969, he became President of the National Coursing Association (NCA), and one of the first board meetings he called was to discuss the sensitive matter. "Rabbit coursing is done," he told the members. "It may be three years or five, but it's done." He proposed that rules be written for the Nationals to be held on an oval track with a mechanical lure. There was plenty of grumbling from old-timers who'd grown up with coursing and believed they had a right to continue the practice at meets. They grumbled even louder when told the Humane Society of the United States had begun lodging complaints about the use of jackrabbits. Dillon didn't back down. Change was necessary, he told them, to preserve the future of Greyhound racing. Before the board meeting was through—and after much heated discussion—Dillon was authorized to write up the rules for a new kind of meet. He proceeded, knowing that it was the right thing to do. At the next National, the new rules got their first test on Ken Hutchings' nearby training track. A new meet—and a new era—was born, fostering other changes, as well, such as the National Coursing Association (NCA) changing its name to the National Greyhound Association (NGA) to more expansively reflect what the group represented. Along with track racing, lure coursing continued at the meets until 1978 when the Association could no longer sanction jackrabbit coursing under any circumstances.

An incident Dillon had with the great sire Downing underscored how problematic the practice of jackrabbit coursing could be. After retiring from racing in 1979, Downing, was syndicated and stood at stud on Dillon's Olathe farm. It would be fair to say that this Greyhound out of Hookers Flower by Big Whizzer was a living legend whose talent did much to attract positive attention to the sport. For example, millions of people watched the television replay of Downing winning the 1977 Hollywood World Classic. Widely circulated *Sports Illustrated* ran an in-depth feature about him, one of two articles the magazine would run on the canine star. While the dog's racing career was managed with shrewd flare by Jim Frey, Downing proved he was worth the hype. In his book, *Great Names in Greyhound Pedigrees*, Gary Guccione remarked that Downing was "near-faultless on the track— a true racing machine." Indeed, he was a record breaker who could take his winning ways on the road. He captured the Hollywood World Classic, the Hollywood Futurity, Biscayne's Irish-American, and Wonderland's Battle of Ages. In addition, he secured the 5/16 Black Hills record and the 3/8 record at Taunton. His track accomplishments earned a rare honor when the American Greyhound Track Operators Association named him Captain of 1977's All-American team and the NGA's members voted him run-a-way recipient of the Rural Rube Award.

The "racing machine's" superiority transferred to the breeding arena. Managed by Dillon, Downing remained in the top-10 sire standings from 1982 to 1986, holding court as top producer from 1983 to 1985. It wasn't all numbers, either. Downing's quality flowed to his descendants. He was a champion who produced champions. For all his distinction, though, Downing was, first and foremost, a dog spurred by canine instinct and genes. Although Dillon himself hadn't used rabbits for training since 1972, some folks still did. One fellow who lived in Missouri drove about 400 miles to pick up his jackrabbit supply every week or so. Dillon suggested the fellow meet the delivery truck at his place to shave off about 200 miles, plus save fuel and mileage. The fellow thought this was a great idea, and soon called to ask if it would be okay to meet the truck at Dillon's place that weekend. Dillon said he would be away at Southland in Arkansas, but indicated the exchange could be made in his driveway. When Dillon returned home, he assumed all had gone well with the transfer of jackrabbits, and he didn't think anymore about it.

The next morning he decided to exercise the senior Downing before he worked pups in a grassy field on his property. It was the middle of summer, so he wanted to get all the Greyhounds exercised before it got too hot. Dillon and Downing had just begun a light work-out when up popped a jackrabbit to Dillon's surprise and dismay. In a flash, Downing gave chase, trying to snatch the rabbit in his jaws, which he couldn't do because he wore a muzzle. On his 3-wheeler, Dillon tried to get between the two, but couldn't. He hollered for his helper to bring him the shotgun, which the boy did—gun in one hand, single shell in the other. Dillon loaded the shell, aimed at the rabbit, shot, missed. "Bring me a dog," Dillon shouted. "Which one?" the boy called back. "Any one of the old bitches. Just hurry." By then, 8-year-old Downing wheezed hard with fatigue, but he kept on, not about to stop with a rabbit on the loose. When the boy brought out a Greyhound without a muzzle, Dillon let her loose in the field. In seconds, the jackrabbit was caught, the chase over. Downing, meanwhile, was in bad shape. "If I hadn't been exercising him along, the chase would have killed him right then and there," Dillon said. To get Downing cooled off, he hosed him down, gave him a shot of whiskey, and kept him moving in a slow, steady, walk. He also put in a call to Missouri. "Did one of those jackrabbits get loose?" he asked. "Yes," came the reply, "But [the rabbit] went out into the field, and I figured he'd be okay there."

After supper that day, Dillon had to go to a bank meeting, so he settled Downing under a big shade tree to rest. During the meeting, a loud banging began on the bank's exterior door, continuing nonstop until someone went to find out what was going on. It was Viv in tears. "Downing's dying," she cried. "Tell Keith that Downing's dying." Dillon got home as fast as he could. Sure enough, the dog was near death. Dillon's vet was out-of-town, but he knew of another. He tried getting the phone number, but when that didn't work, he jumped in his car and went to the vet's house. "Doc," Dillon said, "Downing's dying sure as the world." In short order, they had transported the nearly comatose Downing to the vet's office where the two men tended him for hours. Finally, at 2 a.m., the vet looked over at Dillon and said, "Keith, I think we're going to save him."

Later that night—by then it was almost dawn—Dillon took Downing home and settled him inside the house. The dog required medication every couple of hours, and he was so sore that Dillon had to carry him outdoors to relieve himself. For two days and nights, Dillon remained by Downing's side, determined to nurse the venerable sire back to health. Whenever it was time to go outdoors, Dillon tapped Downing lightly on his side. The usual response was a thumping of the tail that said, "I'm ready." Once, about 3 a.m., Dillon tapped, but the tail remained still. "Okay, Downing," he said, tapping again, "Let's go." No response. Dillon lifted the dog's head. Nothing. Refusing to accept the possibility that Downing was dead, Dillon tapped again, this time on the dog's chest, directly over the heart. The tap was delivered with assertive conviction that resolutely willed the dog to respond. Suddenly, Downing jerked out of a deep sleep, instantly alert. "When [Downing] raised up and looked at me like he did, I knew he was going to get well," Dillon remarked. He was right, of course, but his prediction made sense. Downing, like Dillon, was stalwart in perseverance, strong in constitution and determination. There was simply no way the Greyhound was going to let a jackrabbit get the best of him.

Downing, though, was not invincible, and time plus age proved tougher than jackrabbits to conquer. It is said that for every birth, there is a death, and this was true in the case of Keefer and his grandfather. On the blustery January morning of Keefer's birth, Downing was failing. Two months later, on the Ides of March, his ninth birthday, Downing died. When Downing closed his eyes for the last time, Keefer wrestled nearby with his siblings, blissfully unaware that the baton had passed and settled itself squarely on his long, strong back.

CHAPTER TWO

*"If you think I can go
to St. Pete and Southland
with the big boys, I'll do it."*
—Jim Schulthess

Jim Schulthess (right), winner's circle,
Tucson Greyhound Park, 1972.

Jim Schulthess and Perceive, 1981 All-American.

Crazy Leap

While Dillon battled freezing cold in a thick jacket, gloves and boots, Jim Schulthess padded around in tennis shoes, tee-shirt, and Bermuda shorts. On his way to the kennel that January morning, Schulthess yawned and lit a cigarette at a stop-light. He fiddled with the radio dial, searching for a song to soothe the headache pounding behind his eyes. The partying had gone on too long at Dave's Aqua Lounge the night before. It was all Randy Blair's fault with his endless jokes and pranks. The miniature frog in the gal's drink was the kicker. She was so drunk, she didn't even notice it swimming in her vodka gimlet. He stopped the dial at the golden oldies station. Simon and Garfunkel crooned, "Bridge Over Troubled Water," and Schulthess felt like a cool cloth had been placed over his eyes. The song reminded him of his wife. Jane was his bridge, his best friend, the mother of his girls, a terrific teacher, a trooper through thick and thin. She was goddamned perfect, except when she wasn't like the night before when he stumbled in at 3 a.m., and she gave him a general's cussing. Crap, he deserved it, too. The partying was going to stop. He'd promised her and he'd promised himself. It was too hard to get by on a couple hours sleep anymore. He felt every inch of his 38 years, especially when Stephen Stills pounded out, "If you can't be with the one you love, honey, love the one you're with." Shit. He switched off the radio as he pulled the dog truck into the kennel's parking lot.

Ennis had already mixed feed. The Greyhounds had been turned out and were back in their individual crates awaiting breakfast. Schulthess eyed the bloody mix of meat, biscuits, and vitamins, and felt like puking. He steadied himself by looking at the race form to refresh himself on which dogs were racing that night. Yes, he had a strong string of Grade As, as always, but nothing like the stellar line-up he'd had in 1982, all from Dillon's farm. Damn, that was the year to beat all years. Perceive, Understood, Bold Footprint, Havencroft, Position, Preview, Spirit Start, Widdy, Whiffen, Dunrovin, Benji's Alibi, Visible, Wind Hitter, Searail, Privilege, Byword. He could recite the list sober or drunk, backwards or forwards.

Perceive, his all-time favorite, led the pack as the most consistent sprinter ever to race the Derby Lane-Southland circuit. Ninety-eight wins and hardly ever an injury. Perceive had stamina and smarts. He outwitted top competition time and time again. Without a doubt, the dog could've snagged 100 wins, too, but that would have meant dropping him to Grade B, and there was no way that was going to happen. Schulthess retired him instead, so Perceive could be remembered as the first class champion he was, not some tired challenger slipping down the grade ladder into the fair-weather pool.

"Don't feed Havencroft, Dunrovin, and Widdy," he said. "And make sure you weigh each and every serving." That last was a jab at his assistant who was a stickler, a cook that never took his eyes off the recipe kind of guy. It had to be done the same exact way each and every time. Schulthess believed in perfection, but you had to have a little flexibility in life. Hell, you couldn't rely on the adding machine all the time because you'd forget how to count.

"Keith called," Ennis said as he plopped a dollop of feed into a stainless steel pan. "Wants you to call him back right away. Said he's got something important to tell you."

Schulthess nodded and walked outside to sit in the sunshine and have a smoke. He didn't want to talk to

Dillon until his headache was squeezed down to a nub. His partner was not an idle chatter. On the phone, Dillon's words tended to sound severe and clipped, like he was pissed. Not true, but his calls always had sharp-arrow purpose, and you had to be prepared to respond with purse details, injury reports, rehab schedules, inch-by-inch race results. Dillon was one of the smartest men Schulthess had ever met. A goddamned genius. Year after year, the old veteran raised no more than 30 pups, and year after year when Schulthess took them to the track, most ran to Grade A and stuck. It was Schulthess' job to keep them there. He liked the challenge, and he liked the income. A 50/50 split with Dillon on the purse earnings amounted to a nice chunk of change when you ran mostly Grade As and stake winners like Perceive, Position, Understood, and Havencroft all in the same year. Damn, he missed Perceive, the crème de la crème as far as Schulthess was concerned.

Ennis appeared at the door. "Keith's on the phone," he said. "You'd better take it."

Schulthess frowned. His headache had shifted to the top of his head, which felt like it was going to blow a gasket. "Did you tell him I was here?"

"I sure did."

That was the trouble with efficient help. You couldn't get away with anything. If Schulthess hadn't hired Ennis himself, he would have suspected Dillon had sent him as a skulking sentry.

"Hey, Keith, it's 78 degrees here. What's the thermometer say in Olathe?" Schulthess liked to poke weather fun at Dillon, especially in January when Kansas was particularly bleak. More to the point, he wanted to ward off questions that his throbbing cloud of a mind couldn't answer just then.

Dillon bypassed weather chat all-together. "Say, I got you a champion today. A pup out of Perceive and Position. I tell you, he's going to do it all."

Schulthess wondered if Dillon was addled by the cold. It was not like him to gush over a pup, newborn or otherwise. He always played his cards very close to his chest.

"Keith, I think there's a bad connection. Can you say that again?"

Dillon repeated what he'd said word for word, speaking clearly.

"Perceive?" Schulthess said, stuck on the word. He'd been ruminating on his favorite Greyhound, wishing he'd had him back. Now, this.

"Perceive's pup."

Schulthess still wasn't sure that Dillon was okay. Maybe his age was finally catching up with him and he was having a lapse of good sense. Still, it would be nice to have another superstar like Perceive.

"He's the one," Dillon said.

Schulthess waited for Dillon to shift into question-asking mode, but all he said was goodbye. The phone went dead.

"Want to help me here?" Ennis said, waving his hand like a student trying to get the teacher's attention.

"Sure," Schulthess answered, his headache gone. It was going to be a good day. He could feel it. Instead of grilling, Dillon had offered good news, which surely meant Jane wouldn't leave like she had threatened the night before. It was a leap of odd logic, but somehow it made perfect sense following Dillon's own leap into the fray.

Jane had threatened to leave before, and she hadn't done it. He could understand why she wanted to leave a dozen years earlier when he told her he was quitting law school to train racing Greyhounds. That had been a crazy leap if there ever was one, but it had been the leap of his life. He had never regretted it.

Schulthess had been briefing a case at the University of Arizona law library when he glanced across at one of his classmates who pulled out a race program instead of a law book. He didn't know the guy very well, but Schulthess whispered, "What the hell are you doing?"

The guy grinned. "Me and two of my buddies tell our wives we're going to study at the library and we go the dog track instead. Want to come with us?"

The brief wasn't finished, but after three semesters, Schulthess was bored with scribbling notes and trying to make sense out of endless tangles of legalese. His only hesitation was a guilty moment when he thought about Jane teaching typing to put him through school. He knew she relished the moment when her husband, the lawyer, would bring home the first of many fat paychecks. Well, one night at the races wasn't going to put a crimp in her dream. He might get lucky, even if he didn't know the first thing about reading a race form.

"Count me in," Schulthess said, closing his law book.

At Tucson Greyhound Park that night, Schulthess saw racing Greyhounds in action for the first time. One thing Kansas didn't have in the early 1970s was a racetrack where parimutuel wagering was legal. Growing up in Haven, Kansas, he knew there were Greyhound farms in the state, but he'd never been to one. He was aware that Abilene, Kansas, was headquarters for the National Greyhound Association, but that fact barely registered in his mind. He knew about coyote bounty hunters who got as much as $50 for every coyote their Greyhounds chased down. But, coyote chasers might as well have been ambulance chasers compared to the sleek, muscular, beauties he saw sprinting around the oval after a mechanical lure.

His bets that night in Tucson were safe show wagers that meant he won money if his picks ran first, second, or third. For almost every $2 bet, he made a profit of about 60 cents—certainly paltry compared to what his classmates wagered—but he liked the constant cashing in and getting something back race after race. Instant gratification suited him much better than slogging through law books night after night. The betting was a kick, and he congratulated himself on being naturally good at it, but what he really liked was watching the Greyhounds. He couldn't believe that any animal was capable of moving with such precision and grace. The "poetry in motion" cliché had to have been penned by someone who watched Greyhounds move. And, from what he'd heard, Greyhounds racing at Tucson were the has-beens and never-will-be racers that couldn't make it at the more competitive tracks such as Phoenix, Portland, St. Pete, Boston. He didn't believe that Greyhounds could be any more impressive than these, but he wanted to find out. In fact, before the night was over, he knew that law school was history. All he had to do was find a job working at a kennel, and, of course, break the news to his wife. Starting out, he'd scoop shit all day if he had to. He knew Jane would throw a raft of it at him. She was not going to understand that he'd discovered his niche at a run down race track in South Tucson.

He was right. Jane didn't like the information. Clutching their young daughter, she had eyed him like he was a rattlesnake about to strike. She wasn't one, though, to sit still for fangs to sink into her flesh, and silence was not her weapon of choice. She chose her words carefully and volleyed them into his lap, a shuddering grenade.

"If you go into this, you are going to do it without me. I'll leave."

Schulthess didn't want to lose his wife and daughter, but his gut told him he had made the right decision. He was not backing down. If he'd had a stash of money, he would have put every nickel of it on his choice. All to win. No show bets for him in this.

Within days, he was hired to mop up at the Carl Pritchard Kennel. Earning less than a mini-mart clerk, his job involved hosing, scraping, scooping, raking, and scrubbing. Anything that involved piss and shit, water and slop involved him. Clorox was his best friend for sanitizing every surface. He quickly realized that the racetrack was glitz and glamour compared to kennel work. Despite the dish-pan hands and stiff back, Schulthess preferred what he was doing over legal mumbling and wrangling. Being around the Greyhounds was bonus enough. When Pritchard sent his trainer to another track, he offered the vacancy to Schulthess who accepted, but joked later that, "the entire operation was put under my incompetence." Still, he did plenty right. As the 1972 season ended, he lifted the kennel from last to fifth in the standings. Best of all, Jane hadn't left. Perhaps she understood there was no swaying her husband from the biggest gamble of his life.

With that notch on his belt, Schulthess accepted a summer training job at South Dakota's Sodrac racetrack. His wife and daughter accompanied him. When Sodrac ended, the family returned to Tucson so Jane could resume her teaching post. Schulthess brooded on what to do next.

Like most tracks at the time, Tucson and Sodrac were sea-
sonal, allowed by law to race only a designated number of
days each year. When a typical 60-day meet ended, kennels
had to follow the racing circuit, which often resembled a
pinball machine: Arizona, Oregon, Colorado, Florida,
Massachusetts, South Dakota. Mix and match, mix it up.
Inevitably, a move was involved. It was a gypsy life that
Schulthess wasn't sure he wanted, especially with a family.

Before the year was out, he took another stab at a more
conventional lifestyle, one that didn't require disrupting
his family every four months to traipse to a different track.
He accepted an instructor position at Kansas State
University in Manhattan, which just happened to be about
40 miles from Abilene and its many Greyhound farms. The
family moved there to settle in for the long haul. Jane landed a teaching job in the Little Apple.

Consciously, Schulthess set the Greyhounds aside, but
he couldn't erase them from his mind. His KSU job
involved traveling from town to town teaching govern-
ment officials and their staff how to handle disasters.
Neither he nor his pupils mustered much enthusiasm for
the topic. Soon, he found himself taking detours to visit
farms surrounding Abilene to get his Greyhound fix. Visits
weren't enough. In relatively short order, he heard about
ten sandy acres for sale on Abilene's Greyhound Road,
aptly named due to the Greyhound farms lining its edges.
The land's price was right at $200 per acre, but Schulthess
didn't have two nickels to rub together, let alone a down
payment. His desire to get back to what he loved spurred
him to sniff out loan opportunities. Before long he had borrowed funds to buy the land as well as a house trailer to settle on it. He'd gained approval for loans to build fences and

shelters. Best of all, he had Greyhounds in his life again. Breeding, raising, boarding. Since Greyhounds were his primary focus, it didn't matter to him whether he was racing or raising them. Although he kept his "day" job at KSU, his heart and mind belonged on the farm. His detours increased in frequency. Instead of blathering about disaster preparedness, he communed with Greyhounds, which was just the way he liked it.

When Schulthess had a problem he couldn't solve, he went to Wayne Strong, a Greyhound man who lived nearby. Strong, in fact, was influential in bringing Dillon and Schulthess together. Strong needed marathon Greyhounds for racing in Florida and he heard Dillon might have one or more. When Schulthess' job took him by Dillon's Olathe farm, he decided to stop in. Although it was dark, and Dillon could have no idea who was knocking, he flung open the door like he'd been expecting someone. Perhaps, he had a premonition. He told Schulthess he didn't have a marathon dog just then, but he expected to have one soon. Later, when Dillon heard through the grapevine there was a "new kid on the block," he'd already met him. Schulthess, in turn, could say he had met the legendary racing veteran he'd heard so much about.

Before long, Dillon made arrangements to bring Schulthess a litter of year-old pups that needed finishing touches to make them track ready. Dillon did most of the training on his farm, but he didn't have a training track where he could teach the Greyhounds to "turn left" as they must on racing ovals.

"Keith brought those dogs to me in Abilene," Schulthess said of the 250-mile trip. "It was the only time he ever did. From then on, I had to meet him half-way. He hated to spend any more money than he had to. Really, though, he wanted to check my place out—to see if it was clean and the Greyhounds healthy. He didn't have to worry about that. When it came to kennels, I was a clean freak."

With Dillon satisfied that Schulthess' housekeeping skills were adequate, a deal was struck. Except for one small hitch. Schulthess told Dillon he'd have to pay the board in advance. Dillon looked at him and said, "What?" By then, Dillon had been an established pillar in Greyhound racing for nearly 40 years. His reputation was solid. Schulthess later joked that it was like asking Rockefeller to pay for his gas before he pumped. The request had nothing to do with trust, and Schulthess told it like it was—he needed an advance because he didn't have enough money to buy supplies or meat. Dillon could have turned around then and left, taking his Greyhounds with him. He didn't. Perhaps he saw something of his own youthful self looking back at him with a 'you just try me' attitude. In any case, Dillon took a chance.

After Schulthess finished that litter and returned it to Dillon, he got a call. "James," Dillon said formally, "I have these pups back that you did and they're fancy-looking. I've got dogs at the track that don't look this good."

Although Schulthess replied, "Thank you," he wasn't sure if Dillon was offering a compliment or giving him a subtle hint that something was wrong. He didn't know Dillon well enough yet to know that when he said something, he meant it straight up.

When Schulthess called him back for clarification, Dillon laughed. "If you're doing something good, you ought to hear about it," he said. "That's why I called."

Several litters later, Dillon asked if Schulthess would consider returning to the racetrack. Schulthess said he didn't know. His farm was beginning to prosper. He had the trailer outfitted to live in and he could finally pay his bills each month. Business was good. Dillon told him that if he did decide on a return to racing, they could partner 50/50 with Schulthess managing the track kennel and Dillon supplying the Greyhounds. The percentage split was more generous than most. It basically meant the two would be equal partners, not owner and hired help. Even so, Schulthess leaned towards staying with his farm. To get an objective opinion, he went to Wayne Strong for advice on what to do. Strong looked at him and said, "You either get in your truck or run to call as fast as you can and accept Dillon's offer."

Arrangements weren't sealed on the phone. It was the kind of exchange that required face-to-face discussion. They took a ride. Driving on a country road, Dillon asked, "What are you going to do?"

Schulthess hesitated. Strong had more-or-less ordered him to say yes. Acceptance would mean he would have to give up his farm. It was a hard-scrabble place, but it was his—and Jane's. Together, they built it into something. He knew it would only get better. His racing experience was limited to short seasons in Tucson and Sodrac, rough and tumble places themselves. He'd never even been to the big-time venues where Dillon's Greyhounds competed.

"Well," he said, not sure what the rest of the sentence should be. "If you think I can go to St. Pete and Southland with the big boys, I'll do it."

In typical minimalist language, Dillon replied, "You just take care of the Greyhounds." He could easily have added, "We'll figure out the rest," because that is what he meant and that is what they did.

Indeed, the Dillon/Schulthess combination was a

powerhouse to be reckoned with from the beginning. Schulthess' first season began at Derby Lane in January of 1976. Strategies were mapped out in daily telephone conversations between the two men. Schulthess did a lot of listening because he understood he could learn a great deal from Dillon who'd been a "dog-man" years before Schulthess was born. Dillon's kennel standing had always been among the top ten, and Schulthess wanted to keep it that way. In fact, he wanted to nudge it all the way up and let it hover there. With such high-caliber stock, there was the challenge of nurturing ability already in bloom. Keeping the Greyhounds interested, motivated, and healthy was key. Schulthess liked to joke that what he mainly had to do was stay out the way and not mess the Greyhounds up. That, of course, was partially true, but definitely not the whole story. His management was crucial.

After a year of the Derby Lane-Southland circuit, Schulthess began to believe he could not only run with the big boys, but beat them big-time. Typically, he had no more than 35 Greyhounds in his racing kennel with the male/female ratio evenly split. In horse racing, males and females generally run in separate races to assure level racing fields. Such a division is not necessary with Greyhounds since the two sexes are equally matched. A determined female can steer past males and females with see-ya-later ease. Economy, in 1977, was a good case in point. She was not frugal with her talent, spending all she had every time she raced. In *Great Greyhound Pedigrees*, Gary Guccione points to Economy as "easily the most famous sprinter sired by [Dillon's] Dillard." He reports that she won 8 of 19 at Southland in 1977, won the 1978 Southland Au Revoir Stake, the 1979 Derby Lane

Inaugural and All-Star Kennel Preview, 11 of 25 at Derby Lane in 1978 and 9 of 29 in 1979. She also made the finals of the Biscayne Open in 1978, ran third in the King & Queen at St. Pete in 1979—the same year she set a 5/16 track record at Derby Lane. When she retired, she went back to Dillon's farm and produced like a champion. Out of her breeding to Downing came Dillon's speedster Understood.

In 1980, long distance runner Position revved up. Dillon believed she was the best of many fine racers sired by Dillard. Position's mother, Abella was no slouch, either, having claimed the winner's spot in the prestigious American Derby and earned All American status, setting the bar high for her offspring. Certainly, Position's record speaks for itself. She was 11-2-3 in 25 starts at Derby Lane in 1980. That year she figured in Derby Lane's Distance Classic and finished second in its Derby. She won Taunton's prestigious American Derby and was named to the All-America team. In 1981, she captured the St. Pete track title with 15 wins, again making the Classic finals. Position broke a Derby Lane record at the 3/8 distance. When she retired from racing, the capable router was mated to Downing's son Perceive. The pairing produced do-it-all crowd pleaser Keefer.

Besides Economy and Position, Schulthess managed Position's sister, Visible, who was often in the photo for first. In 1980, Visible set a track record of 31.98 at Southland, won 9 of 23 at St. Pete and 9 for 26 at Southland the same year. This was a gal who lived up to her name.

Beginning in 1982, there was also fiesty Havencroft, a female out of Gimme One by Downing, whose blazing rookie year set her on the path to fame and glory. Starting

at Derby Lane, she won 12 times and claimed the Gold
Trophy Juvenile Stakes. At Southland that year, she garnered 22 wins, including the Au Revoir Stakes, which
made her track champ. In 1983, she grabbed the win title
at St. Pete with 15 victories, then went on to shame the
competition at Southland with 26 wins in 34 starts,
including a blistering win streak that saw her steal 12 in a
row. Such accolades earned her a position on the 1983 All-
America team. Her career closed out with 82 wins against
major competition. While Havencroft didn't mind stealing
races as easy as you please, she wasn't about to let anyone
steal her dignity in the kennel. Watch out if she felt she'd
been wronged because she would inform you with sharp
incisor teeth. Schulthess had the slash wounds and the
swollen hand to prove it. This was a female whose theme
song could have been Aretha Franklin's, R.E.S.P.E.C.T., a
golden oldie with as much fire as Havencroft had in burn-
ing up the track.

And these were just the females!

With Schulthess at the racetrack helm, the Dillon
Kennel remained consistently among the top ten in kennel
standings in the Derby Lane/Southland circuit. In 1978,
the partnership climbed to second position; by 1980, it
was first in victories. The year 1981 found the kennel top-
ping the money won list. With a long roster of champions
in 1982, the Dillon/Schulthess combo won what
Southland's publicist/announcer, Kip Keefer, referred to as
an "unbelievable—definitely unprecedented—170 races."

Five years into his tenure with Dillon, Schulthess was
on top of the world. Tucson's law library hulked in his
memory like a jilted lover, the Kansas farm pouted in the
dusty corners of his mind. Not yet 35, he earned far more

money than he would have as a young lawyer. His family, which had grown to include a second daughter, lived the good life in a spacious home in upscale Barclay Estates near Derby Lane. His neighbors were Weavers, members of the family who owned the track. He definitely had it all.

In the boom year of 1982, Schulthess splurged and bought a Jaguar Coup. Cobalt blue, beige leather interior, 12-cylinder engine. No doubt about it, this baby had power. But, it wasn't just about power; it was about power and elegance wrapped into one classy package that served as a metaphor for the stellar Dillon Kennel as well as a symbol of personal achievement.

Schulthess didn't take that achievement for granted. One night, track star Havencroft slit her left eyelid on the rail, which was where she liked to run. When she came off the track, Schulthess could see that so close to her eye, it was not a cut he could sew up. If it had been somewhere less delicate, maybe, but not there. A trip to the all-night emergency clinic was called for, so he got the Jaguar and proceeded to help her into the passenger seat. Someone remarked, "You're putting a dog in that car?" Schulthess turned to the questioner and said, "Who the hell do you think paid for it?" As the gleaming jewel of a car pulled away, Havencroft settled in for a ride fit for the imperial queen she was.

CHAPTER THREE

Perceive knew these things because he was a watcher, always had been. Rushing headlong into anything wasn't his style. Too fast too soon was definitely not for him.

Perceive's retirement ceremony at Southland Greyhound Park, 1983. Jim Schulthess (behind Perceive) is flanked by Keith and Vivian Dillon.

Perceive

As Position gave birth to Keefer, the newborn's father, Perceive, lounged in the warmth of the kennel at Dillon's farm. Earlier, the stud had a quick romp in the snow, trying mightily to lift all four feet in the air at once so as not to touch the cold stuff at all. Snow was nice enough to look at, but try running in it, try walking in it, try anything at all in it and you just wanted to rush inside and curl into a ball. Still, when personal nature called, you lifted your leg or squatted as necessary regardless of desire. With its bone-chill factor so high, the day had certainly deviated from the usual schedule of turn-out, exercise, feed, a little hanky-panky that felt darned good—it had to do with artificial insemination you heard the boss man say— then, well, then another turn-out followed by a nice long nap.

On a snow-packed day, you'd expect everyone to be thinking along the lines of cozy slumber, but, no, the boss man had snapped a leash on that pretty little Position gal and walked her out of the kennel, who knew where. She'd obviously been getting way more than her share of feed because her belly had more pudge than any self-respecting Greyhound should ever have. It happened to a lot of these gals when they retired from the track. Really let themselves go. On the other hand, sometimes they'd leave with a pudge and come back slim as slim. In such cases, the boss man settled a pack of mewling pups next to the thinned down miss and she'd nose each one, making sure the whiners smelled okay to her. Next thing you know, she'd flop down and all six or eight or ten of the little suckers would be latched on to her undercarriage. She'd sigh and gaze up at the ceiling, no doubt wishing for a knucklebone to chew on.

Perceive knew these things because he was a watcher, always had been. Rushing headlong into anything wasn't his style. Too fast too soon was definitely not for him. Truth is, you could get hurt if you launched too quickly into action. It was definitely best to know what you were getting into on the track or in the kennel. You could learn a lot by watching and one thing he didn't want to do was get around grumpy Dunrovin if he was in a bad mood. That fellow had a nasty snarl and snap that could cause some damage. His temper kept him from making friends, but it didn't stop him from snagging a finalist spot in the 1982 Gold Trophy and the 1983 Festival Stake at Derby Lane. And about moving too fast, too soon, Understood could tell some stories. That half-brother of his didn't know the first thing about watching or waiting. His style was all pell-mell-get-outta-my-way-I'm-coming-through. The boss man claimed Understood was the fastest dog he ever saw, and that terrific speed won him 15 in a row at St. Pete. He took after his daddy, Downing, that way. He took after his ma, Economy, too, when he broke the Derby Lane 5/16th track record that she'd set. Thirty-four wins in 49 starts in less than a year. Nice while it lasted, but Understood had to retire and drag around a broken hock in a splint, thanks to his lack of strategy. Speed, yes. Strategy, no. Strategy: surely the most important word in the universe. Humans who didn't believe Greyhounds knew anything about strategy didn't know anything about Greyhounds—okay, some Greyhounds.

Perceive glanced at his ailing daddy, Downing. Now that he was preparing to depart this earth, the old guy didn't care a whit about strategy, but he'd known all about it when he was king of the track. Or so Perceive had heard through the gossip mill. The story went that his daddy had shamed everyone that challenged him, winning by colossal margins. Long or short, Daddy could do it all when asked.

Daddy. It seemed that everyone around had Downing for a daddy. All the quality racers, that is. Perceive liked to think he was the favorite son, the smartest son, the son who raced smarter and better than all the rest. Ninety-eight races he'd won, two short of the magic 100. Well, 98 was magic enough. Most Greyhounds only dreamed of such a number. Even Pops couldn't match it with his 35 wins in 48 starts. A broken hock took Daddy-o off the track and into breeding where he produced winners, easy as you please. But, nobody—not Downing, not Understood, not Dunrovin—held up like good son Perceive, the 98-race winning wonder, the one who could go back out there and do it all again if given the chance. No strains, no snaps, no arthritis, no aches, no pains. A little age, maybe, but the kind that eased wise into wiser. Yes, he could do it all again, as good as before. Better—if better was even possible. Perceive had never bragged at the track, but at the kennel what could it hurt, especially when all the Greyhounds around him were sleeping? His only competition was the radio pouring out a melody as smooth as the fur on a Greyhound's back. Perry Como, now there was a singer to ease one into a sweet dreamy snooze.

Rolling over on his back, Perceive's eyes drooped in lazy slits, his legs churned in air. Suddenly, he heard the squeak of the lure, smelled other Greyhounds in the long dark box, heard them bark, felt his own cold nose push against the closed metal door. He waited, anticipating the rush, the chase that would begin in the next moment. He was ready.

CHAPTER FOUR

The "Roaring Twenties" era produced
a pressing need for entertainment venues
caused by a streaming influx
of visitors and new residents.

Derby Lane, 1925.

Derby Lane

As newborn Keefer hunted for a teat, Derby Lane dozed. It was midday, the rare time when silence reigned at the racetrack in St. Petersburg, Florida. Earlier, the grounds had hummed with people operating vacuums, floor polishers, weed-choppers, and hedge-trimmers. A tractor had rumbled around the racing oval towing equipment that groomed the silt-sand surface. Now, after morning's work was done, the grounds settled into coiled quiet, waiting until evening when show time came again.

While the exterior slumbered, the interior buzzed. President Arthur V. "Art" Weaver dictated a letter in his office; publicity director Jay Black conducted a telephone interview with the local newspaper; selectric typewriters clacked, copy machines whooshed, telephones jingled. The scene could have been business as usual anywhere. It was, however, business as usual at the world's oldest continuously operating Greyhound racetrack.

On the day of Keefer's birth, Derby Lane was celebrating the beginning of its 59th season. As always, the granddaddy of Greyhound racetracks was guided by its founding family, the Weavers, led in the beginning by Thomas Lee (T.L.) "Dad" Weaver, who was born in Georgia in 1870. The Weaver's did not set out to become racetrack operators. In fact, they came to the sport in a round-about way via timberland holdings and lumber operations.

In 1890, T.L. and his brothers, Sam and John, formed the Weaver Brothers Lumber Company, overseeing operations of a small sawmill in northwest Georgia. In time, they sold the mill and purchased a portable sawmill. The portable sawmill provided flexibility, so they soon pushed into Alameda, Alabama, where they operated a larger mill for five years.

At the turn of the century, T.L., who was by then a husband and father, settled his family in Natchitoches Parish, Louisiana, where he opened a sawmill at Weaver Spur. With his brothers over the next five years, he set up four more mills in the surrounding area, establishing Weaver Brothers Wholesale Lumber Company in Shreveport.

In the early 1900s, the Weavers and T.L.'s brother-in-law, J.H. Loughridge, formed the Weaver-Loughridge Lumber Company. Expanding into north Florida, the group purchased expansive land tracts populated with pine forests. To support burgeoning growth of the company, the family also financed construction of a mill and the company town of Boyd, Florida. In 1921, the Weaver-Loughridge enterprise bought the Pinellas Lumber Company, a retail lumberyard in St. Petersburg, Florida, further expanding their business and land holdings.

The decade was one of change on a corporate and personal level for T.L. In 1923, he moved his family from Louisiana to St. Petersburg, Florida. He also became a widower at age 53 after 26 years of marriage to Mary Elvira Loughridge, mother of his six children.

As his personal life teetered in flux, T.L.'s business life soared. The time was right for company expansion since the sunshine state was gripped by a land and construction boom that produced major demand for building materials. The "Roaring Twenties" era also produced a pressing need for entertainment venues caused by a streaming influx of visitors and new residents. So it was that T.L. led a group of St. Petersburg businessmen in financing a team of

Greyhound racing promoters who built a track on Weaver-Loughridge property with lumber purchased on credit from the family's Pinellas Lumber Company. One expense led to another, and before long the original promoters reached a financial crisis, ultimately defaulting on their debt. The default caused track structures and property to revert to T.L. and company.

Although the entrepreneurial Weaver had no intention of becoming involved in racetrack management, the responsibility fell into his lap when the original group failed. Never one to let an investment falter, T.L. embraced the challenge of managing an entity he initially knew little about. What he did know was business and the importance of service. That knowledge was to serve him—and the new venture—well.

Soon after the track's inaugural on January 3, 1925, T.L. settled into his role as president and general manager of the St. Petersburg Kennel Club, which would eventually be called Derby Lane. Capable support included T.L.'s son-in-law, John E. Brooks, and brother-in-law, J. H. Loughridge, as directors. In time, T.L.'s three sons—"Tubby", Otto and A.D.—would join the operation, as well, with each learning the business from the ground up, running concessions, working in the money room, and elsewhere to prepare them for managerial positions later on.

The ship was launched and on its way. For the next 22 years, T.L. would steer the sometimes wobbly, but always sound, vessel through the Great Depression and World War II. Although he retained lumber holdings in Louisiana and Florida, much of his effort and energy funneled into making Derby Lane a first-class model of excellence.

Through it all, T.L. never lost sight of the bottom line. During the early years of Greyhound racing, seasons were short, lasting about 60 days. Rather than let the facility idle, earning no keep, he opened the door to other entertainment, such as stock car races and an exhibition football game featuring football hero Jim Thorpe. When live races were underway, he assured that celebrated sports stars such as Babe Ruth, Lou Gehrig, and Walter Hagan were appropriately honored when they visited the track to watch the Greyhounds compete. T.L. was an unassuming individual, but he understood and encouraged marketing opportunities that kept crowds happily coming back.

As World War II escalated in the early 1940s, "coming back" grew to be financially and logistically impossible for many folks due to rationed gas. To compound the situation, bus service ended before reaching track grounds. Rather than buckle to difficulty, T.L. found a way to defeat it by arranging for horse and mule drawn wagons and electric motorized carts to transport people from the bus stop. Patrons liked the special treatment. They also liked the track's entertainment that provided a break from the heavy weight of wartime, a welcome respite boosted by the possibility of wager luck. Besides the excitement of racing, there was a festive musical group perched in the infield blaring energetic marches as Greyhounds paraded before the crowd.

In 1947, at age 77, T.L. acknowledged his advancing age by passing the day-to-day leadership to his son-in-law, John E. Brooks. He became Chairman of the Board while Brooks assumed the presidency. As the 1940s closed, the pair decided on the next big step, which was major expansion of the facility to accommodate a burgeoning post-war appetite for entertainment. A state-of-the-art steel and glass structure was erected for the then enormous sum of $750,000. It was an investment worth the risk, a last hurrah for the patriarch who was awarded top honors by the Greyhound Writers of America for making "the outstanding contribution to Greyhound racing in 1950."

When T.L. died in 1952, Brooks added general manager to his title. His list of qualifications prepared him for the escalating role. Although he was born in Ypsilanti, Michigan, he had come to St. Petersburg in 1924 during the Florida land boom. As a broker, he sold the land on which the track was to be built. Instead of taking a real estate commission, he accepted stock in the project. When the group bailed out, he remained a board member and, later, secretary-treasurer. In the 1930s, Brooks expanded his horizons in Greyhound racetrack management. During Derby Lane's "off-season" (summer and fall), he served as general manager of the Crescent Kennel Club in Springfield, Massachusetts. Later, he also managed the track in Taunton, Massachusetts.

After seven years, Brooks' dual role as president and general manager was cut short with his death in 1959 at age 68. Brooks' widow, Joyce Weaver Brooks, daughter of T.L., continued with her self-appointed role as goodwill ambassador for the racetrack. For over 50 years, she never missed an Inaugural, and she never stopped serving the track's patrons with her warm and friendly demeanor. Well into her 70s, "Miz Brooks" walked the plant every night showing an interest in everyone she encountered. When she could no longer traverse the expansive grounds, she greeted visitors from her table in the Derby Club. Her sisters and sisters-in-law joined her often. According to

Louise Weaver, Assistant Vice President and Historian of Derby Lane, women of the family could not officially be employed by the track or the lumber company. They were welcome to sit in on board meetings, but only if they remained silent. That rule would change in time.

Upon John Brooks' passing, Tubby Weaver, oldest son of T.L., quietly assumed the presidency. When he died in 1968, second son Otto became president for five years. Youngest son, A.D., followed in the position from 1973 until his death in 1979. Despite having four different presidents in less than 20 years, transitions were smooth due to each brother's long familiarity with the organization. The brothers, though, were in their sixties and seventies by the time they stepped into the presidential post, and age caught up with each.

Still, management remained steady, and Derby Lane hovered confidently at the top of its game. In fact, the facility bulged with so many patrons that a second major expansion was commissioned and completed just before the 1971 season. The expansion enlarged the plant so it could accommodate over 10,000 fans comfortably. Until then, the record one-night paid attendance was 8,821. In 1986, Keefer's presence at the Distance Classic would blow attendance to a record high of 12,779.

The Weavers understood how to please the public, but they also understood how to please kennels that signed on to race at their track. Through the years, clashes between management and kennel operators erupted at other facilities, with disputes usually centered around purse pay-outs. Kennel operators invariably felt they weren't paid enough—often they were correct. At times, such as the late 1950s and mid-1970s, disgruntlement escalated to the point of kennels refusing to race unless purses were increased. Issues never seemed to completely resolve, and ill-will often lingered for months or years afterwards. Dillon himself was caught in a boycott at Miami in the late 1950s that sent him and other kennels scurrying for placement all over the country. Strife broke out in Arizona, Colorado, New England, and some of the Florida tracks, but never at Derby Lane. In fact, kennels were generally so content with purse structure and all-around conditions there that once they landed a contract, operators did everything they could to assure its renewal season after season. With a limited number of kennel slots, competition was fierce at the St. Petersburg track. The joke went that an operator had to retire or die before a kennel had a chance at joining the elite roster. It was close to the truth. Occasionally, though, openings occurred through attrition or expansion. At such times, it was imperative to have a strong kennel of quality Greyhounds capable of running with the country's best.

Dillon secured his first contract at Derby Lane for the 1968 season that began on January 4. He was up against such notable names as Alderson, Kulchinsky, Moses, Castellani, Block, Mamino, Groves, Henry, Whitehead, Thomas, the majority being future Hall of Famers like himself. A few of the kennels had double the number of Dillon's 30 Greyhounds, but most were in that same range number-wise. At Derby Lane, quality over quantity reigned.

When the last of T.L.'s three sons died, the presidential post became the next generation's responsibility. Tubby's son, Arthur V. "Art" Weaver, at 54, had enough years and experience to fill the vacancy. He slipped into the role with the seamless precision that had become a managerial trademark in the family-run enterprise. Art's experience at the track started during childhood. After squeezing oranges at age ten to sell at the track's concession stands in 1936, he progressed to help build the Derby Lane grandstand and work the racing surface before moving indoors to other projects. These hands-on positions prepared the third generation Weaver for the challenging operational duties that awaited him.

Beginning his fifth season as president, Art would have interrupted his dictation to take a call from Dillon had there been one on the day of Keefer's birth. He would have listened intently to Dillon's confident prediction, thanked him for the news, inquired about his family, then bid him a gracious goodbye. With the phone in its cradle, Art would have mentally filed the information and returned to the task before him. First things first.

Meanwhile, back at the Dillon kennel in Olathe, Kansas, Keefer stretched his limbs in lazy contentment after nursing. Curling close to his mother's belly, his mind drifted into the safe womb of sleep. That he would become Derby Lane's darling in two short years was as distant as the Irish fields where his coursing ancestors chased. That he would be the fourth generation of All-American champions was as unimaginable as life without warmth and milk.

CHAPTER FIVE

*With his aviator glasses hiding his eyes
and Hawaiian shirt, jeans, and cowboy boots,
Schulthess looked like a Jimmy Buffet impersonator.*

Jim Schulthess and Havencroft, 1982.

Bonfire of the Vanities

On the day of Keefer's birth, Mike O'Keeffe looked past the enormous man before him and glanced at the clock on the wall. Four o'clock. The guy had a neck the size of most people's waist, or so it seemed in the small quarters of the Tampa Bay Buccaneers locker room. The behemoth had uttered two quotable sentences, all the rest was egomaniacal patter. O'Keeffe thought about the cartoon where the dog hears blah, blah, blah, blah, Rover, blah, blah, blah. That's pretty much what he heard from this linebacker who happened to make a few capable moves in the last game played. It hadn't helped. They still lost and came out of the season two wins, 14 losses. His blahs alternated with the word "me," lots and lots of "me." The chain around his neck was two strands thick. It had to be that thick to hold the weighty gold ingot dangling at the center of his massive chest. The display was conservative compared to some of the glittering treasures O'Keeffe had seen. King Tuts, a whole league of them.

The upcoming Super Bowl in Tampa had hiked the hype to boil-over. Sports talk radio shows were stuck on Raiders and Redskin analysis, stats, predictions. He was so sick of the drivel that he'd tuned in to National Public Radio and news stations for relief. He'd even tuned to a country music station, which was an indication he was desperate because country was not his preference. Still, he found himself tapping his feet to George Strait's Amarillo By Morning, especially the phrase, I ain't rich, but lord I'm free.

O'Keeffe liked football, but lately he couldn't stand the prima donna professional athletes with their obscene incomes. What was it with these guys? He'd rather be on the high school beat again—or, better still, hanging out in the Greyhound racetrack paddock where bullshit was kept to a minimum. He hadn't covered a high school game in years because that niche was reserved for rookies cutting their sports-scribbling teeth. Greyhound racing was another story. Basically, he had it all to himself. When he'd suggested a weekly column, his boss at the Tampa Trib said go for it. No cute or fancy title, either, just "Greyhound Racing" in bold letters beside his photo and name. No gloss, no glitz. The Greyhounds, their trainers, owners, even the track operators at Derby Lane, in particular, were down-to-earth, the kind of people you could have a real conversation with.

The truth was, O'Keeffe had been high on Greyhound racing for years. When he was just a kid about 20, working the sports beat at the Clearwater Sun, a friend took him to the races one night. Something about it tapped the right spot because he was soon writing bits and pieces on the sport, as much as he could for the small paper. After 14 years, he went to work for the Tampa Tribune. No advanced degree ushered him in, either. He'd completed three years of college when the Clearwater Sun's editor offered him full-time work. The job came with the caution that he probably wouldn't have time for school. O'Keeffe didn't wait to find out. He accepted the offer and quit attending classes. No regrets, either. His presence was required at the track to get firsthand information for his Greyhound racing column. He went every chance he got.

O'Keeffe looked at the clock again. Five minutes had passed. This guy was killing him with blather.

"Thanks, man, I appreciate the time," O'Keefe blurted when there was a slight pause in the monologue.

"Call my agent if you have any more questions," the hulk said. "He knows me inside out."

"Yeah, I'm sure he does," O'Keeffe muttered. "Especially your bank account."

Outside, the sky was a bruise of pink and purple when he unlocked his Honda.

Instead of heading to his cubbyhole at the newspaper to tap out a couple of puffed up columns on King Tut, he turned towards Gandy Boulevard. If he hurried, he could catch weigh-in. Schulthess would probably be there with dogs he had racing that night. The Dillon Kennel manager was definitely good for a quote, uncensored, sometimes unprintable, but definitely entertaining.

At the paddock, Schulthess stood in front of the scale with two brindles and a red fawn. O'Keeffe knew who the dogs were without looking at the program. Havencroft, Dunrovin, and Widdy. When you could tell two brindles apart, you knew you were into the thing deep. Not only did he know who they were, he knew their pedigrees. Havencroft's sire was Downing, her dam Gimme One. Dunrovin was her littermate. The brindle pair looked like identical twins. Widdy was a Downing gal, too, and she was more petite and ladylike. "The way a female's supposed to look," Schulthess had said.

Schulthess spotted him and called out, "How's tricks, chief?"

With his aviator glasses hiding his eyes and Hawaiian shirt, jeans, and cowboy boots, Schulthess looked like a Jimmy Buffet impersonator. All that was missing was a cigarette hanging out of his mouth, but smoking in the paddock was prohibited.

"What's Havencroft gonna do tonight?" O'Keeffe called out. Next to some of the other gals, she looked like the jolly giant. She weighed 20 pounds more than most of her gender and her haunches rivaled any males in muscular heft. Schulthess was always quick to praise her determination on the track, but he complained about her masculine features. "I don't want to have to look between a dog's legs to see what sex I'm dealing with," he'd said one night, then added, "Now, don't quote me on that, Mikey. We don't want the public to think badly of our royal miss. She's paying a lot of the bills now that Perceive is retired. Hell, she paid for my Jaguar."

"Win is what she'll do," Schulthess said, attempting to swat a fly with his rolled up program while holding the three leads with one hand. The Greyhounds paid no mind to his flailing gestures since they were occupied sniffing butts in front of them.

"Think she'll make it over to the rail from the 8 hole?"

"Absolutely. Did you see how they wrapped the rail around the first turn?"

"Naw, didn't notice anything."

"Take a look. If she rides it like usual, she won't feel any sharp edges. No trip to the ER tonight. I didn't bitch about the eyelid cut, either. Somebody probably saw the trail of blood and got on it."

Havencroft jumped on the scale without prompting.

"Seventy-two pounds," Schulthess said. "Right on."

"Got a minute?" O'Keeffe said after the last of Schulthess' dogs were weighed in and led to the lock-out kennel.

"Sure, I'll buy you a drink." Schulthess said. "Then, I'll tell you about the call I got from Dillon today."

"I'm all ears," O'Keeffe said, eager for the news.

CHAPTER SIX

*"For five or six generations,
Traffic Officer blood flowed mightily
through every vein of the
American Greyhound's pedigree."*
—Gary Guccione

Traffic Officer.

The Run-Up

One year after Keefer's birth, he and his littermates loped out to the fenced field with Dillon who pulled a square box on wheels. Although they couldn't see the coonskin scrap tucked inside Dillon's jacket, they lifted their noses as if they smelled it. They'd already sniffed the box on all sides. When the box didn't react, they lost interest. For the first time since their birth, Dillon thought the 12-month-old pups finally looked like Greyhounds. They'd lost the last of their baby fat and clumsiness. Now, they floated, their paws appearing to skim rather than touch the earth. Keefer led the way, his siblings following behind. He circled back and nosed Fun Size who pricked her ears, but otherwise ignored him. In the litter of five, Keefer stood out, not just because he was taller and heavier than the others, but because he was the only red fawn among brindles. In size, shape, and color, Keefer resembled Traffic Officer who raced and reproduced during the 1920s and 1930s. It was that resemblance that caused Dillon to remark, "He's the one, Doc."

Keefer and Traffic Officer were both big dogs that weighed five to ten pounds over most males of their respective eras. Keefer's racing weight was 82, Traffic Officer's 76. Each had especially long, strong, backs that helped power them past competitors on short or long stretches. Their racing styles would prove to be similar; if they got off to a bad start, they managed to pick-off competition, one by one, and do it in record-breaking time.

While Downing was Keefer's biological grandfather, Traffic Officer was kin in a more expansive way. Referred to as "the grandfather of the American Greyhound," Traffic Officer was so labeled by Gary Guccione in *Greyhound*

Breeder's Journal because he was the "first great native sire to emerge following the acceptance of the revolutionary idea known as track racing." The red male out of Vixen by Meadows was born in April 1925. His own birth occurred six years after track racing was officially born in Emeryville, California, and four months after Derby Lane's grand beginning. Indeed, as Guccione points out, "for five or six generations, Traffic Officer blood flowed mightily through every vein of the American Greyhound's pedigree."

Before he would prove his merit at stud, though, Traffic Officer accomplished the rare feat of excelling in field coursing as well as track racing. In 1926, the champion-to-be won the National Futurity coursing event over 142 starters. These would have been the best coursers in the land, traveling from all parts of the country to compete. Amazingly, he went on to finish in the money in 95 percent of his track races, breaking records at Chicago, Kansas City, Tampa, Tijuana, and Springfield, Ohio.

Art Wilson, who raced Traffic Officer, was quoted in the *American Greyhound Racing Encyclopedia* of 1963 as having said, "In most of his races, he was last going to the first turn, and on top halfway around the first turn. He'd coast the rest of the way home." Obstacles didn't interfere with his ability or desire to dominate. Nowhere was this more evident than during a race in Springfield, Ohio, where a Greyhound escaped from his kennel and dashed onto the track attempting to catch the lure. Instead of catching it, the loose Greyhound was knocked down, then rose up directly in front of Traffic Officer, who held a two-length lead in the race. "The Officer just hurdled him and went on to win," Wilson remarked.

Dillon was eleven-years-old when Traffic Officer ran his first track race at Tampa in 1926. That balmy state—and track racing itself—was a long way from Dillon's home town of Cedar, Kansas. The young boy, who spent his spare time sweeping up at the local grocer, knew nothing about the fastest dogs in the world. In 1932, when Dillon watched Greyhounds compete for the first time in a national coursing event in Kansas, Traffic Officer was already retired from coursing and racing. By then, he'd been purchased by George Oswald who retired him to stud in California after the dog raced and won against Gold Leaf at Tijuana's Caliente for a $5,000 bet. At the time of "Old Red's" death in July of 1937, Dillon was still a year away from his first experience preparing Greyhounds for the coursing nationals.

Legends being legends, Dillon would soon know about Traffic Officer. Anyone involved with coursing or track racing knew about him. This awareness was to continue for decades to come; in fact, it would exist well into the 21st Century. For good reason, too. The champion's descendants read like a veritable "Who's Who" of the Greyhound Hall of Fame, including Real Huntsman, Beach Comber, Lucky Pilot, Rural Rube, Never Roll, My Laddie, Court Jester, and hundreds of other first-class Greyhounds, each carrying Traffic Officer's blood as well as his desire to compete.

Keefer was part of the high-powered mix. In fact, according to Guccione, Traffic Officer shows up in Keefer's pedigree no less than 30 times! The blend of "Old Red's" blood and the pulsing desire to dominate was a potent elixir coursing through Keefer's body. That desire was apparent to Dillon when Keefer played with his littermates, and during the training process that began with the square box on wheels—the Jack-a-Lure, Dillon's own invention.

With muzzles on, the lanky pups wrestled in a separate pen while Dillon set up the Jack-a-Lure. He attached the coonskin to nylon cord that unfurled from a spool hooked to the square device. Settling the lure in front of the starting box lid, he let out the nylon cord as he rolled the Jack-a-Lure 100 yards away. He made sure the operating battery was clean, then tested the equipment by clicking the push button starter, which also controlled speed. The nylon cord began reeling in, pulling the coonskin along the ground. It scooted across the grass like a live creature. After re-situating the lure, Dillon had his helper bring out two of the pups, Keefer being one of them, Butterfield the other. Dillon stood at a distance, beside the Jack-a-Lure so he could operate the push button control. The pair of pups entered the starting box, not sure what was next, but eager to get back into the light. When the lid lifted, Keefer spied the moving target and sped after it. Butterfield followed after he realized a chase was on. Dillon let them maul the coonskin as best they could with muzzles protecting the product. After several days and five trials with the coonskin dragging the ground, the pups learned to chase the lure as it dangled on a whirligig in the air. They broke from the box and chased the dangling coonskin around a small circular track. Five trials later, they advanced to a larger training track with longer stretches between turns, still chasing the coonskin. Five trips around the training track and they ran unofficial trials at a regulation racetrack. By then, it was the chase instead of the lure that mattered. The lure could be any color or shape. Dillon joked that "a Post Toastie's cereal box" could be attached to the traveling arm and the Greyhounds would pursue it with ardor.

The Jack-a-Lure was a pivotal innovation because it proved to Dillon and doubters that Greyhounds did not require live lures to train into champion racers. His 1972 female Abella, out of Lucky Bannon by Orange Ice, was among the first he trained on the Jack-a-Lure. She handily earned elite All-American status by beating the best in the land when she claimed Taunton's prestigious American Derby in 1974. Her daughter, Position, carried the Jack-a-Lure torch by repeating her mother's performance as an All-American and American Derby winner. In fact, from Abella forward, all of Dillon's Greyhounds were trained on the Jack-a-Lure, including three-time All American Perceive and trail-blazing, record-breaking Understood.

That Keefer and Traffic Officer shared similar traits and talent was particularly interesting because the two did not experience the same conditioning methods. As a coursing Greyhound in the 1920s, Traffic Officer's training and his coursing competition inevitably involved live jackrabbits. In contrast, Keefer would never taste blood, yet he had racetrack stamina and drive to match "Old Red."

Considering the thousands of years that Greyhounds chased prey for food or sport in the Middle East and Europe, it is illuminating to contemplate that live lure use in America was comparatively short-lived. The coursing practice began in the U.S. as a crop-saving/life-saving necessity. Greyhounds arrived in the U.S.A. during the mid-1800s primarily to serve Midwestern farmers whose crops were being destroyed by a jackrabbit plague. The largest and fastest of the hare family, jackrabbits lustily chewed their way through crops. Amazingly, they could match Greyhounds in raw speed, easily running up to 45 miles per hour. To catch a jack in open fields, a Greyhound could generally win if he had the stamina to stay with the chase until the jack wore down, assuming the sprinting hare didn't disappear in a hole or brush.

Farmers were surely awed by the grace, focus, and speed of their Greyhounds in motion. It was the kind of visual experience—a show, really—that one could not ignore. Soon, the show expanded beyond work into entertainment. Families gathered on Sunday afternoons to let their Greyhounds compete against each other. Wives set out picnic lunches under makeshift shade canopies, children romped in games of their own, babies cried, grandmother's knitted. While some in attendance bet a few pennies, others simply enjoyed the excitement and camaraderie.

In time, the casual family gatherings evolved into formalized coursing meets with the first held in 1886 at Cheyenne Bottoms, near Great Bend, Kansas. The initial event set off a firestorm of interest, drawing visitors from distant places such as New York, Chicago, Los Angeles, Denver, and Minneapolis.

The Cheyenne Bottoms gathering was the beginning of national coursing meets that attracted hundreds of Greyhounds and their handlers to the Midwestern states each year. Most of the Greyhounds were trained on jackrabbits that ranked with cockroaches and rats in the public's eye. Farmers had an even lower opinion because their livelihood was continually threatened by the prolific creatures that were vile rodents to them. Nevertheless, the goal was to score competitors on the quality of their chase, not their ability to kill. In fact, training facilities and coursing meets were often set up with escape hatches for the jackrabbits.

The meets were so popular and well attended that the need for a Greyhound registry led to the 1906 birth of the National Coursing Association (later to be called the National Greyhound Association). Established in Friend, Nebraska, the Association moved to Abilene, Kansas, in 1945, where it has remained ever since.

When Owen Patrick Smith perfected the mechanical lure in 1919, it was first successfully demonstrated on an oval track in Emeryville, California. Many of the patrons, dogmen included, had just returned home from World War I, and they were eager for diversion. As a synthetic rabbit lurched by with Greyhounds in pursuit, cheers went up. Actually, dogmen might not have cheered since many resisted the mechanical lure with cynical vigor. They were convinced Greyhounds would never chase anything dead, let alone fake. Smith, however, was convinced that a mechanical lure wasn't going to ruin their Greyhounds, and he set out to prove that the chase, rather than the kill, was what thrilled the dogs.

The mechanical lure was, in fact, a turning point invention. It marked the birth of Greyhound racing as it is known in the world today. The sport was born in California, a significant fact at a time when so many peo-ple—and so many things—were born elsewhere.

Smith is quoted as saying he invented the lure, in part, to do away with Greyhounds killing rabbits as they inevitably do in coursing. He wasn't particularly interest-ed in gambling, but he wanted Greyhound racing to become accessible entertainment. He believed in its appeal.

Appealing though it was, Emeryville didn't succeed

primarily because betting was not officially allowed at the Blue Star Amusement Park, and admission fees were not sufficient to cover debt and expenses. The track operated on weekends only, and attendance was low because Emeryville was in the middle of nowhere. This fact is hard to believe today since Emeryville is close to Oakland and the center of San Francisco. In 1919, however, the town was too far out for most people to easily get to. Nevertheless, the track at Emeryville remained open through 1919 and 1920 before closing for good a few days into the 1921 race meet.

Smith didn't let the closing of Emeryville slow him down. With associates in 1921, he opened three new tracks in Tulsa, Oklahoma, East St. Louis, Illinois, and Hialeah, Florida. He opened a fourth track in Chicago in 1922. The tracks struggled through a couple of years, managing to stay open despite low attendance. By 1924, Hialeah was the only one of Smith's four tracks still running.

Hialeah probably would have gone by the wayside as well, but Greyhound racing finally found a niche when night racing was introduced there in 1925. Night racing meant blue-collar folks could come after work. It also meant there would be no competition with horses that generally ran during the day.

Greyhound racetracks sprouted around the country after night racing was introduced in 1925. In fact, the number of tracks increased by 100% that year. Derby Lane was one of the few that would survive decades. Although Smith died in 1927, his wife, Hannah Smith, continued on the path he set in motion.

That path set Greyhound competition on a journey that led away from the use of live lures. While coursing with jacks had its proponents and would linger for years, the practice was ultimately doomed, rejected by the public and, ultimately, its own Association. Never one to idle in the past, Dillon devised the Jack-a-Lure, a viable alternative that he promoted and made available to everyone involved in Greyhound training. In 1978, the National Coursing (Greyhound) Association formally declared that the use of live lures could not be sanctioned for any reason.

The declaration was a moot point for Dillon and, of course, for Keefer who never glimpsed a live jack in his life. It made no difference to him, and certainly did not affect his ability to stay the course, navigating around treacherous turns and powering through traffic to establish and maintain a winning position as he chased a mechanical lure that looked real enough to him.

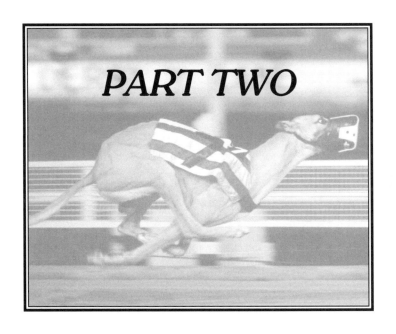

PART TWO

CHAPTER SEVEN

"They schooled that pup that's named after you, and he looks like he's going to be a monster."
—Lou

Keefer in meditative mode, up-close.

Accentuate the Positive

Kip Keefer watched the golf ball sail high into the air until it disappeared in the dense morning sky. The greens unfolded around him like a steam bath, the temperature and humidity thick as gumbo. That was summer in West Memphis, Arkansas, for you. Clothes damp all the time, moist air. He wicked sweat off his face that had pooled and dripped while he concentrated on positioning his body for the swing.

"Not bad, Kip, looks like you just missed the rough," Lou quipped. "Saved again. Say, they schooled that pup that's named after you, and he looks like he's going to be a monster."

Kip nodded. "I hope he is. We'll see. Southland's as good a place as any to start."

"Pup's all legs," Lou said as he studied his club, appearing to look for answers in the shiny stem. "A slip-slider."

While Lou fiddled to get his stance just so, Kip took a swig of soda and wondered what it was about golf that drew him to the course every Tuesday morning, rain or shine. He loved the mental mind-set of it, the concentration, the way you could lose yourself in the moment, a series of moments, the way you competed with yourself to reach personal best. Accentuate the positive. Be decisive. Swing with imagination. Exude confidence. Combined together, the basic bullet points formed a powerful presentation. It seemed like such a simple concept that ought to be bottled and sold to everyone alive.

Come to think of it, Greyhounds performed the way golf should be played. They weren't preyed upon creatures like horses that ran to flee predators, jockeys, bells. No, Greyhounds broke out of the box to pursue with everything they had. That they didn't catch anything was a moot point. Didn't matter. Time after time, the racers rushed out of the box pumping confidence and pleasure in the chase itself. It was all about process, not end result. Every performance was as good as all the others from a dog's point of view. Rather than fret about what went wrong in the past or what might go wrong in the future, a Greyhound approached each race with exuberance, imagination, fresh-eyed quest.

"Get in the cart, Kip, we've got pars awaiting," Lou said. "You're daydreaming so deep, you didn't even notice my fine shot."

"That good, huh?"

"Straight into the rough, my friend,"

"Sorry to hear that, pal."

"Yeah, me too. Always happens, why should I be surprised?"

While many Southland employees worked their way up from leadout, Kip got lucky and stepped into a position as track announcer at age 23. He'd been coming to the races with his father since high school, and he knew the place well. Still, broadcast journalism was what he had envisioned for himself, not calling Greyhound races. Somehow, though, the race caller's job became available, and when asked if he was interested, Kip replied "Sure!" The reason he did so was unclear, even to him, except that he got a thrill out of watching Greyhounds run. The announcer's opportunity had come first, and he took it. After becoming familiar with the Greyhounds and their kennels, he didn't have to memorize a script. He knew who was who and could easily call out names. He liked the variety of that. He liked the variety of each race setting up and playing out differently. He liked the Greyhounds themselves and the kennel operators. He liked his co-workers, the crowd, the energy. Truth was, he didn't want to be anywhere else.

Nobody told him so, but he was sure he got the announcer's job because he had a distinctive voice that instilled confidence. Accentuating the positive was his modus operandi. Patrons could feel it. Track management could feel it too because his announcer's job soon expanded to include publicity director. Either they were hard up for help or he was good. He preferred to believe good. He was good.

At the track, everything happened live. There was no loud "cut" when lines were flubbed and no repeating a scene that didn't play the way everybody wanted it to. Whatever happened in the first turn—or anywhere in the race—remained in the show—heroic or tragic. The adrenaline pumped when he called races because he had one chance to get it right, just like the Greyhounds had one chance during a race to edge out others in the pursuit.

Kip got so addicted to live action that the very last activity he expected to become involved in was the passive process of writing articles. But, Greyhound racing supplied him with plenty of surprises. Written words poured out of him especially when it came to Dillon-Schulthess champs. It was amazing how fast his sentences grew into paragraphs, how quickly his fingers moved over the Selectric's keyboard. After what felt like seconds, but must have been minutes, even hours, he'd have 2,000 words or more, definitely a complete article. He'd sit back in his chair and read the piece aloud, smiling with satisfaction at how the words brought him back to the exciting moments he'd experienced. It was like going back and recapturing the thrill—and the losses—all over again.

To see {Perceive} purposely striding onto the track and toward the starting box for another jaunt on the Arkansas Course became a biweekly ritual for Southland fans and myself, as Southland's public address system announcer.

Perceive had been the beginning for him, but that article flowed into more articles as Dillon's Greyhounds kept flying—and impressing.

In the kennel, they call her Abby. On the racetrack everyone who sees her run calls her awesome. To the world she is known as Havencroft ... Breaking from the five box quickly, she left the other seven entrants to ponder why exactly they were on the track. At the end, she had finished 11 lengths in front and toured the 1,748-foot Arkansas Course in the time of 31.96. This effort was the third fastest clocking over the distance.

And, of course, when writing about Understood, the words fell from him like a lament.

Ducking his head and driving into the first turn he seemed to misstep. Suddenly the entire field was upon him, but he was untouched. Still striding and running as hard as he could, it wasn't immediately apparent that he was hurt. Then when the rest of the pack surged past him everyone knew. Instead of pulling up at the escape turn, he continued. He ran around Southland's oval for the final time on a badly broken hock. His romp around the track aggravated the injury further but his heart would not allow him to stop.

Now here was Keefer, his own namesake, queuing up. Kip was ready for whatever the Dillon-Schulthess newcomer could give. He hoped it was plenty.

CHAPTER EIGHT

*Keefer would have to perform
to the roar of a packed grandstand
as he learned to compete against the best.*

A view of Keefer's body, au naturel, 1986.

Setting the Stage

A few weeks prior to Keefer's 1985 summer debut at Southland Greyhound Park, Jim Schulthess drove to Springfield, Missouri, to get the youngster from Keith Dillon. Twice a year, the two men met half-way between West Memphis, Arkansas, and Olathe, Kansas. It was a little like Christmas each time because Dillon always had six to eight 18-month-old Greyhounds to hand over, all trained and ready for track racing.

"You'll have to make these do," Dillon remarked during every transfer, tongue-in-cheek because he knew most would rise to Grade A.

When Schulthess saw Keefer, he whistled. "Big dog." Dillon nodded. "Yessir."

Neither mentioned the phone call on the day of Keefer's birth when an unusually ebullient Dillon called Schulthess with his prediction, "He's the one." Nor did the two refer to the Polaroid photograph that Dillon had sent when Keefer was six-months-old accompanied by a note that said, "Here he is." The information buzzed in Schulthess' head as he looked the Greyhound over. Dillon studied the dog like he might study a problem, but Schulthess knew it was impossible to read expressions in Dillon's eyes or on his face. His partner wasn't one to readily display inner thoughts. That reticent trait had been the source of tension between the two on occasion. At such times, Dillon's wife acted as referee, suggesting that her husband call Schulthess to clear the air. Ordinarily, Viv stayed out of the Greyhound partnership altogether. She attended special ceremonies at the racetrack as well as those at the National Greyhound Association and Hall of Fame, but that was typically the extent of her involvement.

"His kennel name is Kip," Dillon said. "I'm sure Kip Keefer will be around to take a look at him before long."

The human Keefer was a Dillon Kennel fan. Since joining the Southland staff in 1981, the announcer and publicist had been documenting the accomplishments of Dillon Greyhounds in effusive articles. Perceive was named an All-American for a third year in a row due largely to Kip's praising accolades. As a thank you, the veteran dog man had promised to name a Perceive pup after Kip. And now, here he was, all 82 pounds of him, headed for the expansive oval of Southland.

When Keefer and the other Greyhounds were loaded, Schulthess expected Dillon to utter his usual, "You'll have to make them do." Instead, he said, "Let me know how he does in schooling."

Back on the highway, Schulthess lit a cigarette and settled in for the long drive to West Memphis. He was definitely ready for another laid-back Perceive whose smart, steady demeanor earned 98 wins. Hell, he was ready for another Havencroft with her durable power that racked up 82 victories. He hoped Keefer was the real deal, and not a counterfeit.

Southland Greyhound Park was a great place for a large Greyhound like Keefer to begin. Wth its wide sweeping turns and a unique "Arkansas Course" that was 98 feet longer than the standard 5/16th mile, the layout gave the clumsy newcomer room to goof. And goof he did as his gangly legs acclimated to racing on a big-time track. "He's like a teenager who has it all, but doesn't quite know how to make it all work together," Schulthess remarked one afternoon as he tried to define Keefer's fledgling style.

Newcomers and veterans alike found it challenging to accrue wins at Southland. With a racing season that spanned from the end of May through October, the West Memphis location was the summer home for premiere kennels that raced during the winter season at Derby Lane, Hollywood, and other Florida tracks. Lanky Keefer would have to step into the big pond to face some of the finest competition in the country. That meant he had to grow into his potential quickly without easing through shallow waters first.

The same could be said for the racetrack itself when it opened in 1956 to much opposition. Local newspaper mavens were so miffed that for years they refused to accept paid newspaper advertisements for Greyhound racing. If the mavens had their way, Southland Greyhound Park would have folded like a flimsy house of cards, but that was not to be. From day one, people flooded the grandstands, flowing in from near and far. They arrived from Memphis, Tennessee, which was a few miles across the Mississippi River and Little Rock, Arkansas, that was 120 miles to the west.

Even the original promoter, Ray Edmonds, didn't anticipate the popularity that drew folks like a magnet. The draw wasn't dampened by his auspicious publicity maneuver that backfired. In *The Road from Emeryville*, Paul C. Hartwell relates that about a year before the track opened, Edmonds decided to stimulate investor interest by staging schooling races for special guests. The racing surface was complete as was a large portion of the grandstand. The event looked like it was going to be a great success— for a few minutes. Disaster struck early when a traffic jam occurred in the first race that resulted in a Greyhound being electrocuted when he was knocked into the lure rail.

Edmonds immediately cancelled the rest of the afternoon and went into overdrive to quash negative press.

Despite the unfortunate accident, Edmonds managed to secure prominent investors, including local business-man, Charles J. Upton, Sr. as well as John Masoni, a founder of the Cavalier Kennel Club in Moycock, North Carolina, a track that had a successful run from 1948 to 1953. Paul C. Hartwell was at a closing night party with his father, Paul Hartwell, in 1957. With the handle reach-ing as high as $175,000 in one night, Masoni had turned to Hartwell Senior and remarked, "I think we've about hit the top. Don't you agree, Paul?" Paul Hartwell, a long-time racing secretary and the inventor of the "Hartwell Grading System," replied, "Mr. Masoni, we haven't even scratched the surface." Hartwell remembers Masoni giving his father a look that said oh well, what the hell do you know. As it turned out, Hartwell's prediction was nothing short of prophetic.

By the time Keefer came on the scene in 1985, pro-moters and operators had changed, but popularity of the racetrack hadn't altered an iota. People continued to stream in like water to the ocean, which meant Keefer would have to perform to the roar of a packed grandstand as he learned to compete against the best.

His first official race—and first win—occurred on July 8, 1985. That sprint was followed by an easy Grade D victory putting him two for two. Stepping up to tougher competition in Grade C, Keefer lost three in a row, prov-ing he was fallible. When he bumped back down to Grade D, he burrowed in and began a win streak—seven of eight. The single loss was a Grade A that he very nearly won.

He was on his way to the Hartwell Juvenile Stakes championship when he got caught in a traffic jam during a race on September 1, 1985. The mêlée jostled him so severely he finished a poor seventh. Even worse, a hairline fracture was discovered on a hind leg afterwards. With a splint in place, Keefer sat out the final weeks of Southland's meet. Keefer's record was respectable, but it wasn't any more impressive than many of his competitors at Southland. The injury didn't help matters. For those who remembered the big red Greyhound, the question was "if" rather than "when" he would race again. Neither Dillon nor Schulthess had a sure answer. Sitting calmly in his kennel, watching everything around him, Keefer was cheerful, but mum. He bared his teeth in a broad Greyhound smile, but he definitely wasn't talking.

CHAPTER NINE

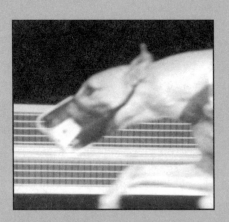

The bottom line was that Keefer
ought to run away with the 61st running
of the St. Petersburg Inaugural, but all the reasons
why he should were also reasons why he might not.

Keefer wins Derby Lane Inaugural, 1986.

Inaugural

S chulthess dumped meat into a tub, then dry kibble and vitamin powder that smelled like alfalfa. With his hands squishing through the mess, he sang along with Frank Sinatra who belted out a snazzy rendition of "New York, New York" on the radio. Singing kept Schulthess' mind busy, and calmed some of the tension that skated along his spine like a hot poker. Twenty-eight sets of eyes watched as they always did when meat hit the tub. Most of the Greyhounds were on their feet, heads tilted as if to study the action better, ears propped in alert position. Keefer was the only one who sat calmly in his crate. His eyes were focused on Schulthess, but, unlike his kennel mates, he wasn't expending any unnecessary energy.

Ennis came whistling through the door and gave Schulthess a puzzled look. "What's up?"

"I needed something to do besides pace and fret."

"Okay, I get it now. For a second I thought maybe you didn't like my meal prep skills. Say, isn't a reporter supposed to be here any minute?"

"I called O'Keeffe and told him not to come. I might say something I'll regret if I see it in print."

"Like what?"

"Like, goddamnit, I don't know what, but anything is possible with the state I'm in."

"Like Keefer may break your heart out there on the track?"

"No."

Ennis shrugged. "Don't want him to see your hung-over shadows?"

"Can you get the bowls, please?"

"Jane called this morning wondering where you were."

"That's all she said?"

"Wondered why you didn't come home last night."

Schulthess continued flexing his fingers in the meat mixture. "What did you tell her?"

"I told her I didn't know that you hadn't."

"Thanks, man, I owe you one."

"You looked mighty busy on the dance floor when I left."

"Just a little exercise, that's all." He tapped his hands on the side of the tub, flicking off bits of meat and biscuit. "Take over, would you? I'm going to call Keith and tell him Keefer's looking good for tonight's Inaugural."

"Did you tell him he scorched 30.71 in schooling?"

"Sure I told him. Jane didn't happen to mention whether she was coming tonight, did she?"

"Nope."

"I'll call her later."

"Good idea. She can't give you too much hell if she's at school."

"Amen to that. I'm on her shit list these days."

"Can't imagine why."

"Give Keefer a golf-ball sized bite of the feed. It won't hurt his run any." Schulthess turned to the 10th race in the Derby Lane program. "Seven is a box he likes. Only one that can run with him is SP's Air Wolf. Maybe Cape May Sonny."

Schulthess knew he was overtalking—and overthinking—because he felt anxious. Part of it was due to lack of sleep and opening night jitters, but most of it had to do with Keefer. Sure, X-rays showed the hairline fracture had healed completely after a four-month layover. Yes, his schooling fractions were outstanding, and he'd come off the track prancing like a show pony each time. With the outside post he had, there should be no problem avoiding traffic and the 4-5-6 crunch zone. All indications pointed to the winner's circle on this sixth day of January 1986. The bottom line was that Keefer ought to run away with the 61st running of the St. Petersburg Inaugural, but all the reasons why he should were also reasons why he might not. Hairline fractures were sneaky little bastards that didn't always show up clearly on film, and four months off was too long for some Greyhounds to get their chase back. Schooling was a simulation of the real thing, but not the real thing. Outside post in a 5/16 mile sprint meant more track to cover running wide, or a necessary dive to the rail, threading traffic or beating it, treacherous either way. Meanwhile a rail runner could already be far enough ahead to make mince-meat out of the rest of the field, even a closer like Keefer.

A glance told Schulthess he ought to relax, everything was going to be fine. The Greyhound looked ready for anything. At 24 months, he was just entering his racing prime. He had the pedigree, the power, the push. Oh man, he had everything he needed. But, was it enough? Nine years heading into ten as Dillon's trainer, and Schulthess still had the same sick feeling he got as a wet-eyed rookie before a big race. The only difference was that now he knew the bile would rise in his throat and slide back down without coming up. He knew the shivers would subside the second Keefer crossed the wire, regardless of finish position. Knowing didn't help the feeling that he was about to go before a firing squad, blindfolded, barefoot, nauseous, dizzy, freezing cold. He called the school where Jane taught Business Education and told the secretary he needed to speak to his wife immediately.

"Is it an emergency?"

"Yes, it's an emergency."

When Jane came to the phone, she greeted him with a threat. "We're in the middle of a typing test, this better be good or I'll chop your fingers off."

"Jane, honey, I love you."

"Not good enough, Jim. What is it?"

"Just that."

"You called me out of class to tell me this?"

"I'm not well. I want you to know how much I love you in case something happens."

"Jim, nothing is going to happen. I love you, too, but I'm hanging up now. I'll see you at home after the races."

"It's opening night. You won't be at the track?"

"It's also Monday. I've got school tomorrow. Listen, you'll be fine. Keefer will be fine."

"I love you. The girls, too. Tell them."

"Goodbye, Jim."

The next morning, Schulthess called Dillon at five minutes to seven. He had a thumping hangover, but he felt cheerful, nevertheless. The word would be hopeful—no, the word would have to be ecstatic. The Inaugural had gone well. Keefer's rear leg and stamina withstood the test. Jane had welcomed him into bed, late as it was, and listened as he recounted how the race played out. To top it off, he'd slept better than he had in weeks with his wife in his arms. Sitting at the kitchen table, he drank hot coffee with the *Tampa Tribune* and *St. Petersburg Times* spread before him.

"Hey, Keith, are you up yet?"

"Yes, I am. Been up since 5:30, you know that." He paused, waiting for Schulthess to chip in with the news.

Schulthess made him wait. "Jane says to tell you hello."

"Likewise. Now, what did he do?"

"The sports writers tell it better than I do. Let me read what they say. *Keefer grabbed the center stage spotlight by winning the 61st running of the St. Petersburg Inaugural in a clear, cool evening atmosphere ... SP's Air Wolf and Pecos Rodriguez were at the head of the field when they steamed out of the first turn in the 5/16 mile. However, the outside running Keefer, boxed well in the seven spot, overtook the two as they turned for home and won the world's oldest continuing Inaugural by a comfortable two lengths at 31.12.*"

"Is that how it was?"

"Close enough. Until the last turn, I didn't know for sure if he was going to fire."

"How did he come out of the race?"

"Seemed fine last night. We'll examine him today to make sure. If there's any heat or tenderness in that hind leg, I'll have the vet X-ray it."

"Good man. Remember the note I gave you after Abella lost the Distance Classic?"

"I do. It said, 'Today's defeats will ....'"

Dillon cut him off, as if he couldn't bear to hear the timeworn adage recited. "Just keep those words in mind as the weeks go by. Now, I'd better get back to work."

"Me too."

Dillon clicked off and Schulthess went back to reading the newspaper. He wanted to bask in Keefer's triumph a while longer.

CHAPTER TEN

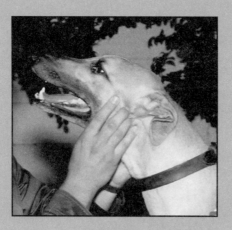

*"I've seen a lot of Greyhounds
in my more than 20 years here, but
I have never seen a Greyhound capture
the imagination of the public like Keefer has."*
—Jay Black

Keefer and Keefer, 1986.

Keefer Fever

The day after Kip Keefer heard that his namesake won the Derby Lane Inaugural, he received a call from Jenny Marriott.

"I need a trainer, Kip. Do you know anyone that might be interested?"

"Let me do some checking and I'll get back to you." He spoke in a calm voice, not wanting his excitement to show.

"Find out as soon as you can," she said. "I'm desperate."

Desperate was a word Kip liked hearing in this instance because it was sure to help his case if he could talk his boss into letting him take a leave of absence. With Jenny desperate, she might consider him for the job even though he had no kennel management experience. As a widow trying to keep the kennel going after her husband's death, she'd want a reliable individual who listened when she spoke. He was definitely the right person for that because he had to listen if he was to accomplish what the job required. He would be all ears, in fact.

Timing was perfect, really, because Southland was in hibernation mode and would remain so until its racing season started in late May. Kip couldn't believe the call came when it did, with him daydreaming at his Southland desk about how he'd like to be at St. Pete for the entire season to watch Keefer perform. The country's granddaddy track was full of luminaries—even more than usual. If he was there, he'd be in the midst of great minds. Besides the Dillon/Schulthess combo, there was the great Irishman

Don Cuddy, who was training for Wayne Strong, Carroll
Blair, R.E. Thomas, Jenny Marriott.

Kip was surprised that Lou Derteen didn't fuss at his
request for five months off. But, then, Kip knew Derteen
always had his eye on the bottom line, and he was probably thinking about the salary savings. Even so, the practi-
cal-minded General Manager didn't want to lose a two-for-
the-price-of-one employee. "Just make sure you return,"
Derteen said in a stern professor's voice. "We want you
back here as announcer and publicity director for the summer meet." He emphasized the dual role to be sure there
was no mistaking what Kip would be doing upon his
return.

Three days later, Kip weighed in Greyhounds for the
Marriott Kennel. He felt like a kid set loose in a candy
shop, definitely the luckiest guy in the world. Being at
Derby Lane meant getting vital racing news as it happened. Southland was excellent, but Derby Lane was vintage, definitely top-of-the-line. Headed by the Weaver
family since opening its doors in 1925, it was the oldest
continuously operating Greyhound racetrack in the world.
Being there meant being an eye-witness to history in the
making.

As days went by, the only time Kip felt a twinge of
conflict—and guilt—was when a Marriott namesake raced
against Keefer. In such cases, Kip outwardly rooted for the
Marriott entry, but inside he shouted for Keefer to gain
another victory.

One of those times was the 25th running of the season's second stakes race, the All Star Kennel Preview, on
January 18, 1986. Keefer was up against Charlie's Babe R,
a petite Marriott female that detested defeat. After win-

ning all three of his Derby Lane races, odds indicated that Keefer would add another notch to his belt. Out of his hat, the 82 pounder plucked his come-from-behind antics as if he was thinking, "Why make it too easy?" He charged out of the one box and burrowed into the middle of the track, settling for third until he reached the head of the stretch. Ahead, Charlie's Babe R hugged the ground, making a commanding move to put the win in her pocket. Keefer wasn't having any of it—he powered up, shortening the gap, chased by a hard-closing Critic. Keefer edged past the leader, winning by a length, with Charlie's Babe R coming second and Critic third. The win made Keefer the champ of the first two stakes races of Derby Lane's season, granting him four wins in four races.

The next time Keefer and Charlie's Babe R met was January 25 in the 26th running of the King & Queen Stake. In that race, the Marriott speed burner dashed into the lead all alone. She outran traffic that bunched up behind her. Keefer, meanwhile, hung behind, managing to survive a first-turn collision. Rallying, he tracked the speck in the distance that was his competition, aiming to overtake the little gal who had acquired a substantial lead in the backstretch. Turning for home, she maintained a healthy gap, but Keefer came on like a freighter, whittling the distance until the very last jump when he nosed past her at the finish line. With six of six wins and all three of Derby Lane's stake races belonging to him, Keefer was beginning to attract substantial notice.

Instead of resting on his laurels, Keefer continued to impress when Schulthess shifted him from 5/16 mile sprints to 3/8 mile routes in preparation for the $100,000 Distance Classic. As it turned out, the 3/8 distance was

Keefer's most comfortable fit. After a couple of 3/8 races that garnered chartwriter comments of "blistering pace" and "increased lead," he was ready for the first round of the Distant Classic tournament on February 7. The chartwriter would note "Early Trouble—Just up," but that abbreviation didn't catch the drama that unfolded. Going into the race, Keefer's main challenger was Carroll Blair's four-year-old veteran, GH's Gator, who typically had no trouble chewing up the competition. In this race, Gator surged ahead leaving Keefer to dodge and weave through crowding traffic. While Keefer fought through one tangle, then another, Gator clipped along with a seven-length lead. As traffic bunched on all sides, Keefer edged his way through with the shrewdness of a chess master, emerging into the backstretch in fourth place. With plenty of ground yet to cover, he made the most of his elongated stride, negotiating around the far turns like a seasoned pro. Heading into the home stretch, a daunting five lengths separated Keefer from Gator who showed no signs of slowing. The finish line was close, time was running out. To Kip—and the crowd—the situation appeared hopeless. This was Keefer's third 3/8 race to Gator's many. The gap between them was psychological as well as physical. Keefer, however, didn't know he was facing an insurmountable cliff. He dug deep inside himself to discover a new gear that urged him stride by stride closer to the charging Gator. As the wire loomed inches away, Keefer burst alongside his elder. The two crossed the finish line together. Silence ensued. The crowd was mute with awe at Keefer's heroic maneuvers. No one could guess what the camera caught. Dead heat? Gator by a freckle? Keefer by a hair? When the judges posted Keefer's number as the victor, the silence exploded into a roar that marked the beginning of frenzied Keefer Fever.

Once started, the buzz bloomed. Crowds poured in to see who the newspapers called, "Wonder Dog." Derby Lane's publicity director, Jay Black, talked Keefer up to anyone who would listen. "I've seen a lot of Greyhounds in my more than 20 years here," he exclaimed. "But, I have never seen a Greyhound capture the imagination of the public like Keefer has." Black's words mirrored those of Keefer fans. Schulthess became a celebrity by extension. As the Greyhound's manager, his comments were quoted with reverential regularity. "I don't know why he is so special, but he's definitely got something," said Schulthess. "Who knows what it is that makes the great ones great? It's just like people. A lot of them have talent and potential but it takes something extra, and he's got it."

Kip soaked it all up. There was no doubt in his mind that he would look back on these months as some of the best in his life—a time when the Keefer glow cast a miraculous spell that was not to missed. He wasn't about to miss a minute of it.

CHAPTER ELEVEN

*On February 22, 1986, the crowd at
Derby Lane hovered just under 13,000,
the largest ever. Keefer Fever was
in full force, everyone wanting
a glimpse of their idol.*

*Record crowd at Derby Lane
for Keefer's Distance Classic win, 1986.*

Classic Fashion

On February 22, 1986, the crowd at Derby Lane hovered just under 13,000, the largest ever. Keefer Fever was in full force, everyone wanting a glimpse of their idol. Schulthess just wanted the race to be over. He couldn't express his anxiety to stoic Dillon who never revealed his interior jitters. For all Schulthess knew, Dillon didn't even have pre-race jitters. He glanced at his partner of 11 years. Straight-back, firm jaw, sealed-together lips, eyes focused on a distant horizon. Who was this man? Besides being a goddamned genius when it came to breeding, raising, and racing Greyhounds, just who was he? Schulthess didn't know. The words that came to mind were mysterious, inscrutable, sphinx. Yes, that's what Dillon was: a sphinx when it came to emotions. Dressed in a plain suit, the man could be on his way to a funeral or a swearing-in, possibly a wedding or a baptism. Dillon's stance and his suit indicated something solemn and formal to be sure: the $100,000 Distance Classic.

Oh man, oh man, Schulthess wished he could fast-forward past the biggest race of Keefer's career. He wished he could slide right on in to the following morning when it would be all over and he could read what happened in the newspapers. That was the kind of distance he wanted, not this interminable period before the 10th race when he couldn't control his nerves. The headlines would scream no matter what, something along the lines of "Wonder Dog Scores" or "Wonder Dog Flops." He just hoped there wouldn't be headlines announcing, "Tragedy in Classic," or "Hero Tumbles."

Schulthess couldn't express his worries to Dillon, but he sure didn't hold back when the journalists came around, especially Mike O'Keeffe, Steve Baal, and even Kip Keefer, who wasn't technically a journalist, but sure knew how to put words together. He wondered if these guys could read his mind because he didn't remember actually saying some of the quotes attributed to him: "I wish the final was tonight." "I just want this one to be easy." "I hope he doesn't put me through one of those nail-biters." "I don't know if I could stand it."

Schulthess felt a nudge and for a second he thought it was O'Keeffe or some other reporter requesting a quotable statement. They'd been thick around him lately, wanting to visit the kennel, get photos of Keefer, find out what and when the champ ate, what his habits were, how he behaved during turn-out, how often he crapped. Win a dozen races consecutively and anything you did was news if you pranced around like Keefer to show off for admirers.

"I said, I'm going to get a soda. Would you like something?"

What Schulthess almost said was "How about a vodka and club soda on the rocks," but Dillon didn't drink liquor and he didn't want to be rude. "A soda sounds good if you can make your way through the crowd."

"I can make it all right, but do you believe all these folks?" Dillon waved his arm to encompass the entire plant: clubhouse, grandstand, exterior, interior, every inch filled by animated people, many of them wearing tee shirts silk-screened with a stretched out Keefer wearing a number one blanket and the words, "I saw Keefer run at Derby Lane."

Schulthess shook his head. "It's amazing."

As Dillon disappeared into the throng, Schulthess looked up at the sky. He couldn't decide if a full moon was good luck or bad. Good for birthing, he'd heard, but also a time for strange occurrences. The only strange occurrence he wanted was that Keefer win his 13th consecutive race at Derby Lane, making a sweep of the season's four stakes races to date. Inaugural. All-Star Preview. King & Queen. Distance Classic. He wished it wasn't his 13th race going for his 13th win at Derby Lane. No one had ever called 13 a lucky number. He'd heard that most high-rises lacked a 13th floor, numerous airports skipped a 13th gate and airplanes had no 13th row. Hospitals and hotels regularly had no room number 13 and many cities had no 13th street or avenue. The thing to do would have been to jump over 13 and call this Keefer's 14th race, but no such luck. Luck certainly wasn't on Keefer's side when he came out of the post position draw with the number four, which was about as unlucky a position as possible. It didn't help that early speedsters, Sir Gallion and Milo's Luck, were on either side of him with burner Stella Valentine, in post number one. Hell, there was plenty of opportunity for traffic problems all around with this line-up, luck or no luck.

The thing that gnawed Schulthess the most—and the journalists had plucked him bone dry with their probes on this prickly matter—was that team Dillon and Schulthess had never won the really big races before. Derby Lane's Distance Classic, Sprint Classic, and its Derby eluded the duo with a slippery vengeance. He thought back over the losses that shouldn't have happened and he felt the pain all over again. In 1976, his first season with Dillon at Derby Lane, their female Abella was the favorite to win the Distance Classic. Nobody thought she could lose, but that's exactly what she did. Second place was as heartbreaking as dead last. Then, there was 1982 when shining stars Perceive and Understood went into the Sprint Classic as "sure-things," only to get shut out by Genes Spur in a bizarre upset. Perceive and Understood went on to beat all others with 19 single season wins each, but it was the big one that Schulthess had wanted and it slipped through his hands like water. Oh man, he could hardly stand it. He wished he could live in the moment like Keefer, or any dog, without the past or the future creeping in to squeeze the present into a worried blob of torment. The waiting, which had ratcheted into minutes before post-time, still seemed insurmountable.

"Here's your soda," Dillon said, handing him a paper cup. "Cheers!"

"Back at ya," Schulthess replied with a voice that sounded weak to him. He gulped the icy liquid, channeling vodka down his throat instead of pop. He might as well let his runaway imagination take him someplace soothing. The bubbles tickling his throat made him feel suddenly giddy and foolish, but also strangely calm. The race was out of his hands. There was nothing to be done.

"I'm ready," Schulthess said. "How about you, Keith?"

Dillon dipped his head in a quick nod, his facial features exactly as they had been all evening. Suddenly, Schulthess pictured the two of them waltzing across a vaudeville stage singing a carefree duet. It was a crazy sight, but it made him smile. Dillon didn't appear to notice the goofy grin stretched across his face. Just as well.

The rumble started in the post-parade with a low-key hum as the first three Greyhounds were presented. Stella

Valentine, Cape May Sonny, Sir Gallion. When Keefer's name was announced, the hum increased in buzz and pitch until applause covered everything—and everyone. Voices occasionally drew above the din to shout his name. Keefer stepped high and playfully tossed his head, his tail beating out a tune, his eyes roving over the faces, seeming to say, "Thank you friends, I love you, too."

At the starting box, his demeanor transformed from frisky to meditative. His energy poured inward, a sucking tsunami traveling to shore. When the box opened, he dealt with the difficult four post by springing to the lead ahead of traffic. He was instantly a coiled rocket, impossible to catch. In the 37.26 seconds it took him to run the 3/8 mile, the question became not if Keefer would win, but by how much. Stride by stride the space increased. Four, six, eight, and finally nine lengths between him and his race mates. Far behind him, Cape May Sonny claimed second and GH's Gator nabbed Sir Gallion at the wire for third.

Stats revealed that Keefer had turned in his fastest time at the 3/8 distance, breaking his own record—and the season's track record—for the third time. Another record was the $112,660 that was wagered on the race, the highest ever at Derby Lane. So many people bet on Keefer that the odds were roughly 1-9, which meant for every $2 wagered, a short $2.40 was returned for the win. With such odds and numbers, the track had to dip into its coffers to cover the difference between what was bet and what was owed in winnings.

When Keefer joined Schulthess and Dillon at the winner's stand, every one of the 12,779 people present thundered with appreciation. Whistling, shouting, clapping, crying, those who were not already on their feet, stood to give him a standing ovation. Draped in a silk winner's blanket, Keefer posed in royal fashion, looking as relaxed and laid-back as if he'd been on a dawdling jaunt through the park.

The next morning, newspaper accounts would capture comments from adoring fans: "We came to see Keefer. I just bet six dollars on him, in fact, and that's a lot of money for somebody on retirement." "[My husband] was in bed and got up just to come for this." "Can't make no money on him, but there's somethin' special about just watchin' him run."

As soon as Keefer jetted out of the box and snared the lead, Schulthess relaxed. All of the tension that had piled inside him like a fortress crumbled into flakes of light. It was as if he could see again. Not only see, but hear, smell, taste. He had his senses back. Later, a reporter would ask how he felt about finally winning the big one, and he'd reply that it felt like a monkey—no, a goddamned gorilla—had been tossed off his back. When he looked at Dillon, he half-expected to see the inscrutable partner he was so used to; the man whose face remained static, unchanging through wins as well as losses. What he saw, though, was Dillon's face cracked in ear to ear grin. Yes, a gorilla shed once and for all. As Schulthess looked into the flashing bulbs, he recalled the note Dillon had handed him after Abella's loss ten years earlier. "Today's defeats will pave the way for lasting victories." Tonight was one of those victories, and it was so, so sweet.

CHAPTER TWELVE

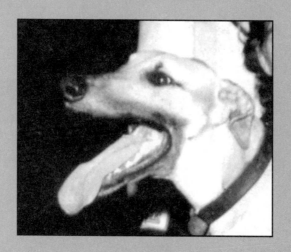

Derby Lane's "Wonder Dog" had slipped.
Instead of extraordinary, he was racing
like an ordinary Greyhound,
losing as many as he won.

Jim Schulthess, Keith Dillon, and Keefer
accepting the trophy for Derby Lane's Distance Classic, 1986

Shock Therapy

On March 3, 1986, Derby Lane hosted the largest Monday night crowd ever. Most were there to watch their darling Keefer race for the first time since his Distance Classic triumph, and they expected him to add number 14 to his list of consecutive wins.

He was coming into the race with eight days rest—just right, some remarked. All wrong, Schulthess said, even though he was the one who decided to give the champ time off to recharge. He had mentally kicked himself for letting Keefer languish after coming out of the Classic in peak condition. Three days, maybe four, but eight days invited an athlete's form to nose-dive. He knew that, so what had he been thinking? Schulthess didn't have an answer. Keefer appeared fine, and maybe he was fine, but a race was the only definitive indicator. This was a 5/16 sprint that would require an adjustment for Keefer after seven races—and seven wins—at the longer 3/8 distance. He had proven he could do both, but 3/8 best suited his come-from-behind style.

So far in the season, Keefer was four for four in stakes wins. One more and he would top the Derby Lane record for season's stakes. If he won a sprint stake in addition to the Distance Classic, he would most likely be the first ever to receive both the Rural Rube and Flashy Sir Awards for sprint and distance accomplishments. As long as he was healthy, the Greyhound had a chance to do what had never been done before. Stakes money was great, but Schulthess wanted Keefer to set records that would take years to crack.

Now, though, as the lights dimmed and the announcer called, "Here comes Rusty," all Schulthess wanted was for Keefer to win his first race following a lengthy layover. A few jumps after the start, the wish converted to a frantic please let him finish without injury. Coming out of the five box, Keefer might as well have been a bumper car. A lesser dog would have given up and dropped out of the knockabout by loping home. Keefer, though, dug in and regained his footing well enough to settle into second place behind SP's Air Wolf. At the far turn, he kicked into high gear for the home-stretch push. Hugging the rail just inside of the leader, Keefer was well positioned to claim the race. Suddenly, Air Wolf veered in his path, causing Keefer to break stride and angle wide. As Keefer attempted to regain momentum, Real Doctor darted through an opening to nip the win. SP's Air Wolf punched in second. Keefer had to settle for third.

As journalist Steve Baal would later report, the loss was "shock therapy" for the crowd that expected nothing less than a dramatic win from their beloved. Schulthess would tell Baal and others that the loss did not concern him. "We were just getting him ready for the sprint stakes. The dog is fine. He'll be back." Despite the bravado, Real Doctor's win created a sick feeling in Schulthess' stomach. That distress, though, was mild compared to what followed when a bug called "jinx" tap-danced in his intestines, flaring nastily after Keefer lost four out of 11 races during March and early April. It was a roiling rollercoaster ride: two losses followed by two wins, then two more losses.

Derby Lane's "Wonder Dog" had slipped. Instead of extraordinary, he was racing like an ordinary Greyhound, losing as many as he won. The chartwriter's superlatives— "scintillating" "splendid" "blistering,"—downshifted to merely commonplace—"driving show," "steady gain," "crowded." People began to murmur, "It's the jinx!"

Schulthess pretended to ignore the whispers, but he could find no viable explanation for Keefer's slide into mediocrity. Physically, the Greyhound was as fit as he'd ever been. He cleaned his bowl at mealtime and happily put on a show for his fans in the paddock and post-parade. In fact, nothing at all seemed out of kilter, except his erratic performance. Was it just tough luck or was the jinx to blame?

The whispered curse floated around Derby Lane like an old, lonely ghost searching for a Greyhound champion to inhabit, especially as single-season win records loomed. In 1939, Jingle Jangle was the first Greyhound to accrue 18 wins in one season's time. Until Perceive and Understood captured 19 wins each in 1982, no racer could break Jingle Jangle's record. Those who got close were foiled in odd, even tragic, ways. Cape Capri had a chance in 1975 after climbing to 17 wins in 1974, but he was deliberately electrocuted by a former associate of his owner. John Denton matched the mark in 1977, but fell promptly into a losing spell. After attaining 19 wins, both Perceive and Understood dropped into a non-win slump—brief for Perceive, but ultimately career-ending for Understood who shattered his right front leg at Southland less than a month later. In 1984, Heartworm matched the 19 win run, but dipped into a losing streak, and died soon thereafter of an undiagnosed ailment. Keefer's slump hit just after he'd beaten the bad luck number 13 by snagging his 13th consecutive win in the Distance Classic. The win series snapped with back-to-back losses followed by a jagged record.

Keefer's fans rumbled, restless with doubt. They didn't want to jump ship, but had the jinx bitten early? Was Keefer headed for the exit?   Schulthess had no direct answers for inquiries, but he was on the hunt for solutions. When it became clear that sprint championships were out of range that season, Schulthess announced that Keefer would race only in 3/8 mile events. That decision proved to be a potent elixir that knocked the vaporous jinx out of sight.

Not only were there no more losses, Keefer raced like a canine Secretariat, winning by double-digit lengths. He made the task look easy. On April 9, he capered to his 18th win, then splashed through mud on April 12 to tie the 19-win record. On that rainy day, sloppy track conditions and a slow start were spurs to his determination that pushed him across the finish line 13 lengths ahead of his competition. His next race on April 16 was a date with record-breaking destiny. His adoring fans clamored to catch a glimpse of their hero. As soon as he stepped on the track to march in the post-parade, rollicking applause filled the air. Keefer pranced and bounced, clowning for his admirers until post-time when he transformed into a bundle of concentrated focus and desire. A hush gripped the crowd as Keefer broke last, then darted to the outside to bypass a tangle of traffic trouble and dash back through a keyhole to ride the rail. He dallied among the competition, but at the top of the backstretch he accelerated with demolishing fervor to claim the lead and surge forward. Any remaining hush in the stands cracked into a roaring deluge as vintage Keefer uncorked, piling 14 lengths between him and the others when he crossed the finish line. With that victory, Keefer established a Derby Lane milestone by capturing win number 20, an unprecedented accomplishment. Already admired and adored, the red Greyhound rose to the level of unmitigated greatness, a stunning composite of grace, power, and performance.

Schulthess was not about to make the mistake he'd made after the Distance Classic. There would be no lengthy rest for the champion. After the race, Keefer's smiling manager remarked, "We're just going to tack 'em on now. He's a great dog and he deserves a place in the history of the sport. We're going to put the record out of reach."

That triumph—and the lead-up to it—caused an explosion of media publicity, including a front page article in the prestigious *Wall Street Journal* on April 16. Francine Schwadel, a reporter for the financial newspaper, was in town to cover a breaking business story, but she heard the buzz about Keefer and followed the trail. She was amazed at the hubbub over a dog. "Suspense is building at the track," she wrote. "Fans mill around the staging area to get a glimpse of what a woman describes as the 'fantastic chest' of her favorite contestant. One man hops around shouting: 'Give me a K! Give me an E! Give me another E! Give me an ...'" Schwadel toured the grounds observing and talking to people there for one purpose—to see the Greyhound they loved as if he was their own. One fan told her, "It's like he's the people's dog." Others offered explanations and excuses for the times he didn't win, defending him like they might defend their children.

The roving reporter discovered Keefer fans outside of the racing environment, as well. Television talk show host Bill Murphy told her, "[Keefer] has a wonderful personality." He came to this conclusion when Keefer was a guest on his television show, "Murphy in the Morning." Sitting next to his canine guest, Murphy told the audience to take a good look. "Is this a face a mother could love?" he asked. Keefer responded by leaning over to lick Murphy's nose. The audience roared with glee.

Schwadel was thorough, leaving no stone unturned. From Kip Keefer, she heard, "You could knock him down and he'd still try to win." Dillon relayed to her that he had recognized the pup as something special the moment he was born. Schulthess struck her as the greatest fan of all— or, as she put it, the most outspoken. "He calls Keefer the best dog in the world," she noted. "And maybe the best dog that ever lived."

Schulthess wasn't the only one to make such laudatory comments about Keefer.

Derby Lane's track president and general manager, Art Weaver, remarked, "I've never seen a Greyhound get the kind of attention he did." Weaver had cause to appreciate that attention because 11 of 13 daily handle or attendance records that season occurred when Keefer competed.

On April 19 and 23, Keefer flashed to wins number 21 and 22, earning chartwriter comments of "dominant" and "preeminent." There seemed to be no stopping the flying ace until jinx's distant cousin, fate, squeezed in with a nagging challenge that put a crimp in the athlete's progress. On April 23, Schulthess sensed something off in Keefer's right front leg after he raced. He didn't limp and he didn't appear lame, but he wasn't 100%, either. Local exam and X-rays revealed nothing amiss other than slight inflammation. Schulthess scratched him from his next scheduled race, April 26, to give him a few days of precautionary rest combined with ultrasound treatment to treat the inflammation. The brief respite seemed to work. When he competed in a qualifying race for the 60th annual Derby on April 30, Keefer performed like he was in perfect condition, capturing his 23rd season win. Staying true to form, he won by nine lengths, earning the chartwriter's remark, "Never in doubt."

As soon as he came off the track that night, Schulthess knew for sure there was a problem because Keefer clearly favored the front right leg. He scheduled an appointment with a top orthopedic specialist in Miami, considered by many to be the best in the country. Schulthess didn't want to take any chances, so he also withdrew the champ from his last two scheduled starts of the season. "He could probably still win the Derby," Schulthess told reporters, "but it's not worth it."

The trip to Miami revealed a tiny bone chip that was detected after a battery of X-rays from a variety of angles. Although surgery was not recommended due to the fragment's small size and awkward position, a heavy dose of rest was essential to reduce tendon inflammation and allow healing.

During the ensuing days, Schulthess made varying remarks to swarming reporters seeking answers about Keefer's return to racing. He was cautious and often ambivalent in his responses: "He's still very young and hopefully has a lot more wins in him." "It's like a football player that gets hurt. They heal differently. Some of them come back and some of them don't." "We hope to get him ready for a major stakes race during the summer." He purposely used the indecisive "we hope" rather than the affirmative "we will" because the truth was Schulthess had no idea if Keefer would ever race—let alone win—again.

PART THREE

CHAPTER THIRTEEN

*Keefer's leg wasn't as swollen as
it had been, and it wasn't quite as
hot, but he still favored it when walking.
Running worth a damn was out of the question.*

Keefer makes tracks north, 1986.

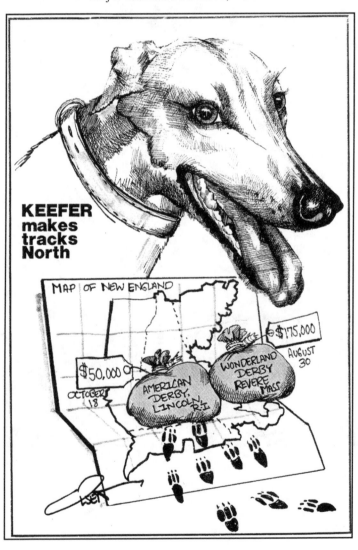

Keefer Has Landed

The Boston Airport was bustling with summer travelers. Schulthess had watched passengers that had been on his flight from Memphis grab suitcases off the revolving carousel and disappear into the throng. His duffel bag was the last of the baggage to spit out of the tunnel, and it looked like a wad of chewing gum after being tossed and tumbled every which way. He grabbed the canvas bundle and hurried to the cargo section where Keefer was to be delivered in his travel crate. After the three-hour flight, the Greyhound would be ready to stretch and pee.

Except for a few people milling around looking preoccupied, perplexed, or annoyed, there wasn't much activity in the claim area. Schulthess looked around, but didn't see any cargo. He also didn't see any airline personnel. He looked at his watch. They'd been on the ground 45 minutes. If bags were already out, cargo ought to be, too.

To the person standing closest, he called out, "You waiting for cargo?"

The man nodded, but didn't volunteer more.

"Were you on the flight from Memphis?"

"No, but I'm waiting on cargo that was."

Schulthess looked at his watch. "They sure are taking their time. What are you waiting for?"

"Dead person."

Schulthess thought maybe the guy was joking, but no smile accompanied his dour expression.

"I'm sorry," Schulthess said. "A relative?"

"Nah, I transport dead bodies. That's my job."

Okay, Schulthess thought, we've got dead bodies on the flight. There were probably dead bodies on every flight, but it wasn't something you liked to think about as you winged above the earth in a metal tube. Let's hope one of the dead bodies on this flight isn't Keefer. He looked at his watch again. Geez, he'd shipped Greyhounds before and it had never taken this long. Or had it? Maybe he was being hypersensitive because of who he was waiting for. The past three months had been a waiting game, and now that Keefer was fit again, any waiting at all seemed too long. Schulthess wanted to get his champ acclimated and schooled on the Wonderland track so he'd be ready for qualifying races and the Derby on August 30. There was plenty to get used to: different track, different kennels, different climate, different time zone. The right front leg had responded well to two months of daily walking and casual running with another month of early morning work-out sessions on the track. There had been no signs of soreness for weeks, but Schulthess hadn't pushed him, either. Slow was the operative word. The idea was for Keefer to heal completely before any kind of pressure was exerted. In fact, there had been no official schooling until X-rays were clean from every intricate angle. The waiting had been worth it. When Keefer had finally schooled at Southland in late July, he'd won by 16 lengths. Now, a couple of weeks later, he was at the top of his game. Schulthess believed he had an excellent shot at the $175,000 Wonderland Derby. Keefer was ready to show these New Englanders what a champion was made of. He'd better be. It was no secret that outsiders weren't welcome. Greyhounds and their handlers that shipped in were referred to as invaders.

Over the next half hour, Schulthess watched as a steady stream of the living and dead arrived, then departed. He counted three coffins on hospital-style gurneys—

one bronze, another mahogany, and a plain pine box nailed shut. In various sized crates, two Siamese cats, a toy Poodle, and a Yellow Labrador wheeled past, all looking dull-eyed like they'd been heavily sedated. A rainbow-hued parrot in a thick wire crate hung upside down and exclaimed, "Knock ya dead matey." Two monkeys came next, a pair that should have been sedated because they screeched and knocked their heads against the sides of their crates. Then, there was the ice chest of who knew what—fresh catch of the day, body parts—something perishable nestled amongst blocks of dry ice that sent up misty tendrils.

Still, no Keefer, though. When the crates and dollies stopped coming, Schulthess panicked. He was the only person still standing in the area. The dour-faced man had left with his dead body, and the other coffins had been wheeled off, as well. None of the crated animals were still visible, though he could hear—or thought he heard—monkeys screeching in the distance and the parrot calling, "Knock ya dead matey." Had that strange menagerie real-ly streamed past or had he slipped into a nervous doze? His head felt muddled, but it often did after flying. He hated flying. His plan had been to drive the 1300 miles with Keefer, but he had waited until the last possible moment to make sure the champ was completely sound. He sure as hell didn't want to make the long trip unless Keefer could return home the victor of Wonderland's Derby. Time had run out for driving. A three-hour flight won out over a 20-hour road-trip. Now, he wondered if he'd made the right choice.

Fifteen minutes later, an airline worker wheeled Keefer's crate out. Keefer was standing, his tail knocking against the crate and his lip curled in his trademark smile. He looked fine.

The worker turned to leave, but Schulthess called after him.

"What took so long?"

"We had a lot of cargo today. Some real humdingers, too. Did you see those crazy monkeys?"

"Monkeys, elephants, gorillas, I don't care what or how much cargo you had. It should not have taken more than an hour to bring him out."

The worker shrugged. "It's been one of those days, sir, I'm sorry." The "sir" eased Schulthess' desire to punch the guy in the nose.

If he hadn't been in a hurry, Schulthess would have asked to see the supervisor, but he quickly rolled the crate outside instead. There was a patch of dirt and grass he'd noticed on the way in that would work fine for emergency business. When he unlatched the door, Keefer rushed out, happy to see him. He was alert and cheerful. On the short walk over to the grass patch, Schulthess noticed Keefer's gait wasn't right. At first, he thought the right front leg had relapsed, but then he realized it was the right hind leg causing the trouble. In fact, he walked like he had a sticker in his paw, but when Schulthess checked, there was no sticker. The leg felt hot and Schulthess thought he detected slight swelling in the thigh.

"What in the hell happened to you?" Schulthess said. Keefer answered by lifting his right leg gingerly to pee.

The next morning, Schulthess opened the Boston sports page to headlines that proclaimed, "Keefer Has Landed!" Great welcome, he thought, lousy reception. Keefer's leg wasn't as swollen as it had been, and it wasn't quite as hot, but he still favored it when walking. Running worth a damn was out of the question.

He called Dillon and explained what happened at the airport. "Somebody slipped him a needle, Keith, I know it."

"You're better off to just leave that alone," Dillon said. "Say he got a poisonous bite or sting on the airplane ride. That's probably what it was anyway."

"I don't think so. An abscess usually develops with those, and no abscess is showing up. Keith, I'm telling you, somebody here did not want Keefer to win the Derby."

"Don't go getting melodramatic on me," Dillon said, his voice a firm scold.

Schulthess bristled at Dillon's reprimand. "We're just lucky they didn't kill him like they did Rocking Ship."

"Nobody ever proved that Greyhound was deliberately killed."

"Don Cuddy thinks he was and he ought to know. It's the same damn thing. Rocking Ship was a marathoner at the top of his game. He was setting records and winning stakes all over Florida. Cuddy called him the greatest—bar none. Same as Keefer."

"All that was 15 years ago. Things are different now."

"They may be different in some ways, but one thing's sure. Keefer's chances are zip to nil now on qualifying, let alone winning the Wonderland Derby."

"I think you ought to give him a couple of days, then school him. He might surprise us on this." Keith's voice had softened into one of reasoning rather than command.

Schulthess stuck stubbornly to the topic. "My surprise was when he came out of that box lame. It was sabotage, and if I ever find out who did it, there'll be hell to pay."

"There's no sense making a big circus out of it. Just

remember, when those reporters show up, you tell them it was a sting or a bite and leave it at that."

"I'll school him if his leg comes around," Schulthess said, his voice an unhappy pout. He wanted to beat the crap out of somebody for doing this to Keefer, but he didn't have any idea where to start.

"Jimmy, I've been in this a long time. It's a good sport and Keefer's a fine Greyhound. People love him and they'll keep loving him, but not if this turns into some Hollywood who-done-it. He's above that. We're above that."

Schulthess could think of no response to Dillon's speech. He knew Dillon had an image to protect and Keefer was part of that image. Hell, so was he. There was nothing to be done about it, not now anyway, not unless he got lucky and found out who was behind the skullduggery.

"Gotcha, Keith. I'd better go check Keefer's leg again." He couldn't resist one more jab, a futile punch at air more than anything, but it relieved a little of the tension that had bound him up like a trussed turkey. "The Boston headline was wrong, you know. Instead of 'Keefer has landed,' it should have read, 'Keefer has crashed.'"

CHAPTER FOURTEEN

On September 22, 1986, the headline
in O'Keeffe's column read,
"Odds Against Keefer's Return."
A couple of days later, Schulthess
was reading it over, a little chagrined
at all the verbatim quotes...

Keefer at Dillon's Olathe farm

Reincarnation

In early September, Mike O'Keeffe caught up with Schulthess after morning schooling. He'd heard some rumors about Keefer and he decided to find out as much as he could. In fact, he had decided to spend the whole day indulging in his favorite sport, even though he had a stack of pending articles on professional ball players to finish. He was at his Tampa Tribune desk, wasn't he? Sure he was on the phone tracking Schulthess down in West Memphis, Arkansas, but he'd catch up, even if he had to work all weekend to do it. Nobody was getting shortchanged.

"Hey, Jim, got some time to talk?"

Schulthess knew better than to start in with O'Keeffe, but he was sick and tired of keeping everything bottled up inside. He'd done exactly like Dillon told him to do. Every reporter had walked away with "poisonous sting or spider bite," and that's what had been printed time after time. Most of the journalists had hovered like vultures without really listening anyway, in a hurry to chase after the next story. O'Keeffe was different. He asked tough questions, and waited patiently while you gathered your thoughts. He listened closely when you answered.

"Sure, I've got a few minutes."

"Want to tell me about Keefer?"

The floodgates opened. Schulthess spilled everything he knew–and felt—about Keefer's latest trials and tribulations. He talked with the abandon of a person who has tossed down a double vodka to loosen up, except his only beverage that morning had been a cup of lukewarm coffee. Keefer, he said, had schooled at Southland on September 2 and come up lame the next day in the right front leg, the same leg that had derailed him in the spring. X-rays showed a possible separation, which meant he might never race again no matter what. The right front leg reoccurrence followed the Boston fiasco that could very well have been subterfuge rather than a sting or spider bite. He had no proof, but he was sure somebody got to Keefer with a needle. As expected, the dog schooled poorly at Wonderland, and it was back to Southland for recuperation. The plan had been for him to race a few times before returning to New England in the fall for two other stakes races. With the September 2 setback, though, there would be months of rehab, which meant no racing anywhere. He was frisky and happy, but lame. If recovery occurred, the goal would be to get him ready for Derby Lane, but that was iffy because January was just four months away. Everything related to Keefer's racing career was iffy. They'd spent so much time working him back into shape and then this, another set back, most likely a permanent one.

"Now," O'Keeffe said. "Take a deep breath. Close your eyes. Relax. You've barfed it all out on the table. You feel better. Let's start over and take it slow so I can assimilate what the heck you said."

Schulthess nodded, he did feel better, calmer somehow. With his hands, he rubbed his sore temples, then eased into a sitting position on the cement floor. In the air-conditioned kennel, it felt cool, almost cold. "I'm ready," he said.

"Good. Let's start with the April 30 injury and move forward to today, September 20. We've got five months to cover. There's no rush," O'Keeffe said. "I've got time. I want to hear it all."

On September 22, 1986, the headline in O'Keeffe's column read, "Odds Against Keefer's Return." A couple of days later, Schulthess was reading it over, a little chagrined at all the verbatim quotes, when the phone rang. He expected Dillon, but it was Dillon's wife.

"Good morning, dear, how are you?"

"I've been better, Viv."

"You know how I try to stay out of the way when it comes to the Greyhounds, but Keith is upset about the latest O'Keeffe article, especially the nasty reference to Boston. He won't say anything directly, but I thought you'd want to know."

"I'm sorry I blabbed so much, Viv, but dang, it felt good to get all of that out."

"I really do understand, dear, but Keith doesn't give in to his emotions like you and I do, and he doesn't understand that need."

"Thanks for telling me. I'll know what the cold shoulder is all about next time he and I talk."

"You'll be hearing from him tomorrow, if not later today. He doesn't like anything to interfere with your chats about the racers. And, dear, I do believe he's going to want Keefer here on the farm for a couple of months to see what he can do to build him back up."

"Sounds like a plan. I'll wait for his word."

After hanging up, Schulthess shook his head. Viv was lovely. He appreciated her go betweens, but why couldn't he and his partner talk about these things directly? Their relationship had more prickly barbs than any marriage. Even Jane didn't require a mediator. Disagreements with his wife got hashed over face-to-face no matter how messy. Well, he and Dillon made a good match as partners in

Greyhound racing, even if they couldn't communicate what was really on their minds. Now, if they could just get Keefer back to form.

Keefer's first full day in Olathe started slow. In the morning, he enjoyed sunning himself on the grass outside his kennel. When he grew thirsty, he lazily lapped water from a nearby bucket. If the October sun grew too warm, he sauntered into his kennel and dozed in the dark as easy-listening music played. He walked with a limp and raised his right leg slightly when stationary to keep weight off the sensitive ankle. Just before noon, Dillon led him onto the grooming bench and felt every inch of the compromised leg and paw. There would be no liniment, no anti-inflammatory, no heat, no cold, no wrap. In fact, the only treatment for the ailing ankle that Dillon would administer would be rest applied until Keefer walked with a smooth, even gait. It might be days or weeks before that happened. Only then could conditioning begin.

"Kip," he said, using his pet name for the Greyhound, "You're just going to have to tough it out." Keefer looked at him as if he understood—his brown eyes steady on Dillon's own, his ears flat against his head in submissive mode as if to say, "I'm with you."

While Keefer had nothing to prove in the racing realm, Dillon believed the three-and-a-half-year-old campaigner had plenty of win in him if the ankle healed properly once and for all. Dillon's goal was to get Keefer back to the track in stellar form. It was the kind of goal the veteran dogman liked having, and he carved out time in his schedule so he could work with Keefer one-on-one when the time was right.

On a crisp morning in November, Dillon drove his gas-powered three-wheeler as slow as possible. Keefer strolled beside him on a leash. For the past three weeks, Dillon had been watching and waiting for Keefer to stop favoring the right front leg. The time had come. He watched the Greyhound's gait as he increased the wheeler's speed so that Keefer eased into a steady trot. They went like that for a half-mile. The walk and trot combination became a daily routine to rebuild stamina. Dillon gradually increased the distance until Keefer could log three miles at a fair clip. After each session, Dillon watched to be sure the limp had not returned. Two weeks into the stamina building sessions, he started Keefer on sprints every few days. A helper held Keefer at one end of the field while Dillon went to the other. When released, Keefer covered the 500-yard distance like a raging arrow. For six more weeks, Dillon worked with Keefer daily, combining stamina and endurance exercise. The Greyhound thrived, showing no sign of weakness in the front ankle. In mid-December, Dillon called Schulthess. "Keefer's fine," he said. "I'll meet you in Springfield."

On January 16, 1987, O'Keeffe caught up with Schulthess at Derby Lane after Keefer's final schooling race. The Greyhound had blazed by the competition, running 5/16th of a mile in 30.75. All three of his official schooling races were equally impressive.

"He's running as good as he ever has," Schulthess said. "Dillon pushed him hard and he withstood everything. We both figured there was no point in bringing him back if he wasn't absolutely sound."

O'Keeffe liked to joke that he could always get a good quote out of Schulthess. This night was no different.

Schulthess felt hopeful about the season ahead, and the feelings loosened his tongue as he doled out kudos for Dillon as well as Don Cuddy, the Irishman whose expertise made him a magnet for trainers seeking advice on medical problems.

"[Cuddy] got some stuff from Ireland or somewhere, and it really works great. I tried it on Keefer before he went to Dillon's farm, and I'm sure that helped his recovery. I'd swear by it."

"What's the stuff?" O'Keeffe asked.

"I call it Cuddy's potion. Probably an anti-inflammatory of some kind, but better than what we're used to. The main thing is Keefer is at the top of his game now. He's ready."

Keefer certainly appeared ready to resume his royal post at Derby Lane. Leaving nothing to chance, the big red dog worked the crowd that congregated to honor him during his schooling trials. As far as fans were concerned, Keefer's allure was as potent as ever.

"I've been following the dogs for 40 years," a fan told journalist Steve Baal. "There may have been dogs with better stats, but there has never been a Greyhound with this kind of charisma."

"He's awesome," said another.

"I've been at Aqueduct and Belmont and seen some great race horses," said a tourist and racing aficionado from New York. "But I have never seen people cheering for a workout for anybody anywhere."

Beyond all the talk, a nagging worry persisted in Schulthess' mind. He couldn't shake the thought that while schooling served a crucial purpose, its value only went so far. Keefer was fit, but would his ankle hold during a hard season of rough and tumble racing? The bottom line was this: schooling was not the real thing—O'Keeffe knew it and Schulthess knew it. All the kennel operators knew it. There was no reason to belabor the point. Schooling was less stressful because trainers could request post-position instead of making do with the random assignments that occurred with regular races. Schulthess had requested the eight box for Keefer, and each time, the wide-running champ had triumphed with flair.

O'Keeffe's column on January 19, 1987, contained none of the doubt that Schulthess felt. The headline, "Keefer Returns Wednesday, and He's As Good As Ever," was a litmus test for the article's gist, which was that Keefer's troubles were shucked in the dust behind him. The impressive trial performances and O'Keeffe's resounding build-up prepped one and all to expect nothing less than victory. Victory, though, didn't happen. Instead, Keefer ran third on January 21, the first time in his life he'd been knocked out of the winner's circle in a 3/8 mile competition.

The race played out with Keefer starting slow, like he often did in long races. No problem there. He rallied into striking position and breezed through the first three turns, making the trip look easy. As he ratcheted into kiss 'em goodbye gear, the five-dog, Byron, banged into him, causing Keefer to stumble badly coming around the clubhouse turn. The crowd of 6,448 shouted his name with enormous might as he regained composure and tracked the leaders, but by then the finish line loomed too close. Kercer and Genuine Choice claimed first and second to Keefer's third.

Afterwards, Schulthess' displayed his best bravado as

reporters swarmed for explanatory remarks. He said the loss occurred because Keefer hadn't competed in a 3/8—or any official—race for nine months. "I knew the first two races would be the toughest," he asserted. "[Keefer] doesn't quite have the same home-run finish yet." The bravado extended to looking ahead. "As long as he's not limping," he advised. "I wouldn't bet against him."

Three days later, on January 24, fans took Schulthess' advice by making their darling the runaway favorite. This time, Keefer didn't disappoint. He barged to a romping win appropriately dubbed "crowd pleaser" by the chartwriter. The victory was a tantalizing appetizer—or so folks thought until he lost next time out, on January 28. "Blocked early" was the chartwriter's remark, a viable excuse for any Greyhound except the master overcomer at his favorite 3/8 mile distance. Reporters sought answers, but the normally glib Schulthess remained silent. He could have pointed out that Keefer was a year older, that he'd been off for nine months and might not be the same caliber Greyhound he was the year before, that his right front ankle was vulnerable no matter how sound. Instead, Schulthess avoided the press, especially O'Keeffe. He attempted a stoic Dillon stance, expressing little emotion. For anyone watching, though, the tension he felt was obvious in the hard suck on his ever-present cigarettes. With each furious inhale, the tips flared, miniature bonfire beacons signaling distress.

As if he sensed his kennel manager's anguish, Keefer suddenly, decisively, stopped losing. His timing was impeccable since four of his next five wins earned qualifying points leading into the forthcoming Distance Classic. When the points were tallied, Keefer had far and away the most at 48. The second leading point earner was Oshkosh Unwind with 33. Elite Blondie had 29. The other five competitors had points ranging from 17 to 23. Keefer romped through the qualifying races as if he had a calculator clicking in his mind and a 12-cylinder engine powering his body. Knocked or bumped, he rallied. Squeezed inside or forced wide, he prevailed. Challenged, he flourished. Keefer the King was back, doling out triumphs like candy. Schulthess relaxed—a little.

CHAPTER FIFTEEN

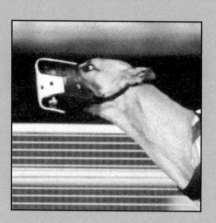

*Keefer shook the barrel and plucked
out a remedy of his own for the situation.
When the box flipped open, he tossed aside his
come-from-behind signature style and
hightailed promptly to the lead.*

Keefer wins Derby Lane Distance Classic, 1987.

Classic Double

After weigh-in on February 21, the night of the 1987 Distance Classic, Schulthess stepped into the paddock bar and ordered a beer. He wore his winner's circle dress jacket, a white shirt, tie, slacks, and cowboy boots, the only part of his attire that he felt entirely comfortable wearing.

A group of trainers were already hunched together in a game of Liar's Poker. Mark Johnson, Clinton Blair, Mark Twillman, Polly Blackwell. All of them had dogs in the Classic. Most had Greyhounds in last year's race, but none had repeaters. Keefer was the only one coming back to defend his title. The poker players thought they had a chance of winning the big race because they each wore ill-fitting clothes conservative enough for the winner's circle or church.

"Get your dollar out and come on over here," Blair drawled. "There's lots of time until the tenth race. Losing money to us now will calm your nerves and prepare you for later."

Schulthess shook his head. "I'm looking for Keith. Has he been through here?"

"Are you kidding?"

"Yeah, I guess I am." Schulthess knew better than anyone that Dillon would go out of his way to avoid a bar. He just wanted an excuse to step in and drink a beer to take the edge off. Lately, he'd been nervous as a cat on the track.

Blair nodded towards the clubhouse and grandstand. "The place is filling up. Probably here to see Keefer get beat."

"You wish," Schulthess said. He knew people were filing in to watch Keefer make history. He wished he could share their blind faith, but blind faith didn't win races. He wasn't about to let these trainers know he had doubts. They'd raze him down to a nub if they thought he wasn't 100% confident. "Just remember, Bennigan's afterwards. Drinks are on me. Get ready."

"That's *if* Keefer wins," Blackwell said.

"A big '*if*' in this mud," Twillman remarked. "Two Step is gonna splash right by your pantywaist runt."

Schulthess laughed. "I guess you're already punch drunk if you're calling Keefer a runt."

"Where's a reporter when there's real news?" Johnson teased. "Say, is your better half coming?"

"He wants to know because he needs a date," Blair remarked.

"Naw, my wife wants to ask Jane about getting a teaching certificate," Johnson said. "Somebody needs to earn steady income in our family."

"She'll be here," Schulthess said. "Up in the clubhouse."

"With Dillon?"

"No, Dillon avoids clubhouse's about like he avoids bars. She's bringing some friends of ours."

"You mean friends of hers?" Blair said.

"No, ours."

"I didn't know you had any friends."

"Like hell. What do you think you are?"

"The competition."

"Yeah, right. You don't mind the free drinks and food when your competition beats you."

"I hate to be rude."

"You just can't help it," Johnson supplied. "Jim, tell Jane that my wife will be looking to pick her brain. Any advice is good advice at this point."

Mention of Jane made Schulthess wince. Damn Xandra in West Memphis. She had her talons in him before he knew what was what, and she'd sunk them deep. Not that he protested one iota. Besides dousing him with flattery, the gal was gorgeous. She'd flown in from Memphis to see him in St. Pete a week ago, and she planned to come back again as soon as he signed a lease on an apartment. He'd inked a lease just a few hours earlier. Soon, he would tell Jane he was moving out.

"Ah, hell, I'm in," Schulthess said, pulling out a dollar bill. Dillon would just have to find him. After the tense lunch the two of them had earlier, Schulthess didn't really want to see his partner again. Before noon, Dillon had dropped his bag at the mom and pop motel where he always stayed, and they'd gone to the fast food hamburger place that Dillon liked because it was quick and cheap. The food was advertised as being fresh and prepared to order. Good value for the money was how Dillon might describe it if he remarked on such things, which he didn't. The man was as parsimonious as a monk, definitely not someone who would order a $100 bottle of wine at a fancy Italian restaurant. Schulthess didn't normally order wine, let alone an expensive brand, but he'd done so with Xandra. Man oh man, it was like she cast a spell over him—he didn't recognize himself when he was with her. It had been like that from the night they met at a party near the Southland track. Their first full evening together had been romantic—the two of them leaning close, candle-light casting sensual shadows, a prelude to later. Well, Dillon wouldn't know anything about such things. He wouldn't approve of them, either.

At lunch, Dillon ate his typical cheeseburger and soda. Schulthess drank a vanilla milkshake, hoping his upset stomach would ease. There wasn't much conversation. Dillon asked about Keefer's ankle, but he knew it was fine because they talked on the phone nearly every day.

"How's Jane?" Dillon said.

"She's great. She'll be here tonight."

"The girls?"

"Fantastic. Doing good in school."

"Everything's okay with the family, then?"

Schulthess nodded, wondering what Dillon had heard.

"I've always liked Jane," Dillon said.

"Me too. Twenty years we've been together." He sensed Dillon was fishing for information, maybe a confession, but the paltry bait wasn't working.

"Viv and I have been married over 40 years and we've never raised our voices at each other once in all that time."

Schulthess stuck a straw in his milkshake and stirred. "You're lucky."

"Very little in life is due to luck, James. Choices maybe, but not luck."

There it was, Dillon's brand of counseling and advice. If Dillon had been a different kind of person, he would have launched into a lecture on right and wrong, moral and immoral, the value of commitment, patience, hard work. Being Dillon, though, he'd leave it alone, let the verbal note settle.

"Look at that rain come down," Dillon said, nodding towards the dark outdoors. "This kind of weather serves a smart Greyhound like Keefer well."

"Intelligence trumps instinct in the rain," Schulthess said.

"Anytime," Dillon said, "But especially in bad weather."

Stormy conditions didn't keep people away from the track. They flocked in by the thousands to see Keefer attempt the impossible. He was one race away from doing what had never been done before by winning a total of eight qualifying races plus the Distance Classic two years in a row. As the Classic's post-parade began, 10,467 fans clamored for a glimpse of Keefer who was wearing the green and white striped seven blanket. As the Derby Lane band trumpeted festive tunes, Keefer danced along the edge of the track, ducking and jiving like a prize fighter approaching the ring. At one point, he tested the surface with his hind feet, sending plumes of mud spray behind him, narrowly missing Seeinandbeinseen, who wore the eight blanket. To most observers, it appeared he was clowning to entertain his admirers, but the trained eye would surmise that Keefer already had his head in the race.

No amount of grooming could squeeze out the excess moisture and muck that rains brought. The sloppy track would slow the field, which could be trouble for speed burners who relied on being in the lead from the start. Slop compromised momentum, and speed was often the first casualty in such conditions. Greyhounds with come-from-behind kick fared better, except they had to withstand mess flying around their heads, maybe into their eyes. If they could bear the debris, they could carve out a win.

Keefer shook the barrel and plucked out a remedy of his own for the situation. When the box flipped open, he tossed aside his come-from-behind signature style and hightailed promptly to the lead. With that burst of speed, he nixed the slow track theory. There would be no wallowing or mud-to-the-eye for him. It was a good thing. As he established a substantial cushion, others in the race knocked asunder in the muck. Number three Elite Blondie and number five Oshkosh Unwind got caught early in a mud-slinging mutual hit. Number six Two Step went wide, but couldn't avoid slip-sliding close quarters that tripped him up. Number one Oshkosh Quick stuck to the rail, but got squeezed into trouble at the clubhouse turn and stayed pinned in sixth place. Marie Shelby gathered her composure for second place, with Kercer and Seeinandbeinseen coming in third and fourth. Keefer won by six lengths, clocking in at 37.69 seconds. In the prior year's race, his 37.26 performance put him nine lengths ahead, but compromising weather conditions were not part of the mix.

As Schulthess and Dillon joined the champ on the winner's stand, Schulthess looked out into the cheering crowd. He thought he saw Jane laughing happily, lifting a glass of champagne to toast Keefer's win. Beside him, Dillon smiled broadly. The smile was out of character, but it looked perfectly natural on Dillon as he gripped the hefty winner's trophy. Even Keefer smiled as camera bulbs flashed. Everybody was happy, except him. What had he done?

After the photographers were finished, Dillon shook his hand. "Good job, James. Keefer's on top of his game thanks to you."

Schulthess smiled, the first real smile he'd managed all night. He knew it wasn't easy—or common—for Dillon to extend such compliments. "Well, we're a team. Keefer, you, me. It took all of us to get here."

"I guess," Dillon said, not one to accept praise with ease. "We're here."

"Will you come to Bennigan's with us?" Schulthess said. "Jane would love to see you."

"I'd enjoy seeing her, too, but I think I'll just go on back to the motel and get some sleep. My flight leaves early in the morning. You give her my regards. She's mighty special."

"You're right about that."

CHAPTER SIXTEEN

Schulthess watched Keefer's eyes as he checked for sore spots. The Greyhound wasn't a yelper, like some, but his body language definitely reflected what he felt.

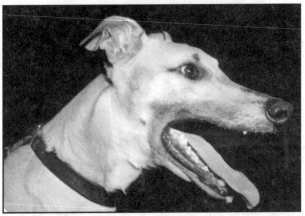

Up-close view of Keefer smiling.

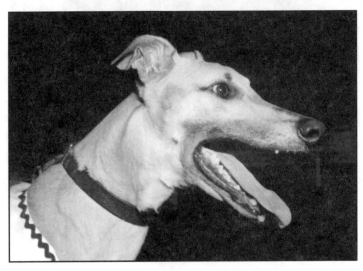

Curtain Call

At the kennel on the morning of March 12, Schulthess went straight to Keefer's enclosure and unlatched the door. "Come on out, big dog, so I can get a look at you. After nine wins in a row, you run second, then third. Something is definitely up." Those were the facts, but beyond them, Schulthess had sensed something out-of-kilter with Keefer as soon as he came off the track the night before. Nothing as obvious as a limp, but a way of walking that indicated discomfort, a shortened gait that signaled distress.

Schulthess watched Keefer's eyes as he checked for sore spots. The Greyhound wasn't a yelper, like some, but his body language definitely reflected what he felt. He showed some stiffness in his left shoulder and flinched when Schulthess pressed the whip muscle in the thigh of the left rear leg. With more pressure, the Greyhound blinked and turned his head.

"The good news is there's no heat, swelling, or bruising, big dog. The bad news is it'll take at least three weeks to heal. You're going to get mighty bored lying around the kennel while the old sartorius mends."

Sartorius was the scientific name for whip muscle, and it conjured images of opulence, decadence, and Xandra. Why did everything remind him of her? She had definite power over him, strange sensual clout that couldn't be rationally explained to anyone. Even he didn't understand it, especially since he knew she wasn't the kind of person he imagined her to be when they met. In fact, he wondered how the hell he could be so good at reading Greyhounds, and so bad at reading women. Experience was part of it, of course. He'd had many years of daily contact with a variety of Greyhounds and very little variety when it came to women. It didn't help matters that he naively assumed all women were as genuine and forthright as his wife. At first, Xandra had reminded him of the actress Ann Margaret because of her voluptuous sensuality. As he got to know her, though, he realized she wasn't sweet and kittenish like he imagined Ann Margaret to be. She was more like the sultry man-eating character Kathleen Turner played in the film, *Body Heat*. He was as big a dupe as William Hurt's character, drawn in by flattery and the woman's aggressive sexuality. She definitively knew how to utilize her assets. Intellectually, he understood that what he was doing was wrong. At times the guilt overwhelmed him. Still, every time he resolved to end the relationship, something happened to curtail what Xandra dismissed as his silly talk.

The sartorius, whip muscle, whatever one chose to call it, was a wily sort. A sore whip could heal with adequate rest. A torn whip was trouble, the kind that lingered indefinitely, difficult to manage with any kind of certitude. A clean bone break was better in a way because when it healed, it healed. A torn muscle wasn't as clear-cut and could nag a lot or a little, you never knew which. It was actually best if the muscle ripped completely in half. At least then it couldn't get any worse.

Schulthess settled Keefer back in his enclosure. "Big dog, your wheels are wobbling. We've got to get them back on straight."

When the kennel phone rang, Schulthess expected to hear Ennis's voice explaining why he wasn't back from picking up supplies. He knew it wouldn't be Jane because she was royally pissed off at him for moving into an apartment. She didn't know about Xandra because every time he started to tell her, his mouth clamped shut out of shame or fear.

The caller was Dillon with a sharp tone in his voice, thanks, no doubt to the gossip mill. "James, I heard Keefer ran third, and he might be hurt. How is he?"

"A little shoulder stiffness and a sore whip muscle, left hind leg. I'm going to lay him up for three weeks, then school him back a couple of times to see how he does."

"Oh, it's not as bad as I thought, then," Dillon said. "Three weeks ought to do it, and still give him about a month of racing before the meet ends."

Schulthess wondered what Dillon had heard—that Keefer had been carried off on a stretcher? He shook his head.

"By the way, how's Jane?"

There he was, fishing again. Schulthess knew Dillon liked Jane, but only recently had she become a main topic of conversation when they talked on the phone.

"She's fine. Working hard as usual."

Schulthess hadn't told Dillon of his move or that he and Jane were separated. He certainly hadn't told him there was another woman. The last thing Schulthess wanted to hear was Dillon's disapproving voice on such matters. With the gossip grinder in gear, though, there was no telling what Dillon had heard or what he believed. Plenty of folks would happily supply information, accurate or not. Dillon preferred to get information from the source, but he seldom asked direct questions about personal situations. Schulthess knew rumors were rampant. They ranged from true to outrageous. Jane had thrown him out of the house / begged him to stay. He was having an affair with a movie-actress / gold-digger / state commissioner / heiress. He was on drugs / in rehab / living in a half-way house / a member of Alcoholics Anonymous / a homeless drunk. He was bankrupt / banking his second million. Take your pick. Some of the rumors were true, some half true, some absolutely not true. The whole thing was ridiculous.

After hanging up, Schulthess squatted in front of Keefer's crate and put his palms flat against the wire. "Big dog, we're a lot alike because my wheels are wobbling, too. In fact, mine are about to fall off."

Keefer looked at him as if to say, "Yeah man, isn't that the truth."

"Anyway, kid, you'll tell me when you're ready to retire, won't you? I don't think this is it, but we're going to take it slow and easy just to be sure."

Schulthess believed a Greyhound's end on the race-track was as important as his beginning. He prided himself on paying attention. The goal—and the art—was to retire Greyhounds at just the right moment. Sometimes that was impossible. Understood was a good example. The two-year-old had blazing speed, but he put extreme pressure on his body by racing all out every time in contrast to Perceive who raced smart, conserving energy wherever he could. The consequence was a shattered hock that ended Understood's racing career far too soon. Sometimes you had to make controversial decisions such as when he retired Perceive two races shy of 100 wins. The Greyhound could easily have climbed from 98 to the coveted 100 if Schulthess had been willing to let him drop from Grade A to Grade B races. Schulthess wouldn't hear of it. He believed Perceive's dignity was far more important than two wins that would propel him into an elite group.

Schulthess had never regretted his decision. Some questioned it, but Dillon had supported him completely. On Greyhound retirement issues, he and Dillon were united.

When Keefer schooled on March 31, he won by two lengths. In his next schooling on April 3, he ran second, a half-length behind the winner. The loss didn't concern Schulthess because it was a 5/16 mile, shorter than Keefer's ideal 3/8 mile distance. When he came off the track, the Greyhound was happy and moving well. A thorough body massage produced no stiffness, no flinches, no awkward turns of the head, not a trace of anything that indicated trouble.

Five days later, on April 8, Schulthess stood between the paddock and the escape where he had a close-up view of the racing oval. It was a middle-of-the-week night with no major races and moderate attendance. It was exactly the kind of low-key program Schulthess wanted for Keefer's debut after three weeks off.

While he waited for post-time, Schulthess mentally listed the pluses in Keefer's favor: the Greyhound practically owned the 3/8 mile at Derby Lane; the shoulder wasn't stiff, the whip muscle was no longer sore; his two previously injured right legs were strong; he had schooled well and come off the track healthy; his lone schooling loss could be attributed to the shorter distance of 5/16 mile. He recited these pluses like a mantra until the lure launched.

Keefer started the race with powerful oomph, but the dynamic changed abruptly a few jumps out of the box when his left hind leg pulled up close to his body, a wounded limb searching for harbor. Schulthess groaned, "Oh shit," hoping for something that would prevent Keefer from running any further. He willed him to be still to stop the damage. Keefer would have none of that kind of behavior. The Greyhound faced adversity as he faced everything else—eyes focused on the challenge before him. In this case, the challenge was to complete what he had started. As the rest of the field drew further away, Keefer slowed to accommodate a three-legged run, which he maintained for a hundred yards. Then, on four feet—far behind and limping badly—he finished the 3/8 mile. Giving up was not in him, no matter the cost.

The silence that shrouded the grounds was louder than any roar. Keefer wasn't used to such a dearth of commotion in his presence. Nor was he used to sorrowful eyes following his every step. He behaved like an earthly saint, limping calmly beside Schulthess into the cool-out area behind the paddock. Even then, when he could have howled in pain, he remained stoic, refusing to indulge in dramatics. Schulthess surmised that the whip muscle had torn. He expected blood to pool muddily under the skin, forming an awkward bruise. On close inspection, he didn't see any discoloration, which meant it might just be a severe pull, something like a hamstring pull in humans. Whatever the damage, Schulthess knew Keefer's moment had come. He would tell reporters that rest and rehab could earn a comeback, but there was no doubt in his mind that Keefer's racing career was done.

CHAPTER SEVENTEEN

*The brass band launched into a festive tune,
pouring into a singular drumroll that led to an
announcer's voice calling out, "Ladies and Gentlemen,
please join me in welcoming the one and only
champion of champions, Kee-EE-fer."*

Keefer wins Derby Lane All Star Kennel Preview, 1986.

Send Off

Schulthess steadied Keefer's head while the track veterinarian, Charlie Murphy, wrapped an elastic bandage around the dog's lower left leg. Neither job was easy because normally calm Keefer fidgeted, wiggled, and whined.

"You'd think we were hurting the boy," Doc said.

"If he was hurting, he'd be still as a post, a model patient. Injections, bone splits, any painful medical procedure and he's fine," Schulthess laughed.

"So, it's just the silly stuff like bandaging he can't abide?"

In answer to the question, Keefer emitted a long, low howl.

Doc patted the leg and stood up. "All done. Let's take a look at our handiwork."

When Schulthess let go of Keefer's head, the Greyhound dived for the bandage and gnawed with ravenous gusto. In seconds, the wrap lay crumpled in a heap.

"That's setting the record straight on who's the boss in this situation," Doc said. "The bandage didn't stand a chance."

"He's going to have to take a bow sans adornment," Schulthess said, brushing Keefer's short fur with his hand. "No bandage, no shiny blanket, nothing but Keefer in his natural splendor."

The bandage had been a doomed idea due to Keefer's refusal to play the role of victim, plus his canine distaste for anything that confined his legs. Doc suggested the wrap as a joke, but also obvious confirmation that a career-ending injury had occurred since no tell-tale signs lingered when Keefer had an audience. In fact, to see Keefer three weeks after the April 8 mishap was to see a Greyhound that looked to be in perfect racing form. Although he occasionally favored the leg around the kennel, there was no trace of a limp when he paraded on the track, no sign of a wandering bruise, no gloomy eyes, hanging head, or tentative step. It was easy to forget his entire racing career had been plagued with nagging injuries that could have slammed the door on his racing days much sooner than they did. Instead, Keefer accomplished what had not been done before—or anytime since—by winning back-to-back $100,000 Distance Classics and all the qualifying races leading up to them. His presence brought 12,779 people to Derby Lane for the 1986 event, an attendance record that would remain intact 20 years later—and probably for all time. With his red fawn coat glistening and his eyes bright with expectation, Keefer looked ready to gallivant and strut, if not race, for his admirers.

The brass band launched into a festive tune, pouring into a singular drumroll that led to an announcer's voice calling out, "Ladies and Gentlemen, please join me in welcoming the one and only champion of champions, Kee-EE-fer."

The Greyhound knew when he was being summoned. Pulling Schulthess along, he leaped and bobbed to the center of the track where Derby Lane's President, Art Weaver, stood with other Derby Lane dignitaries. Keefer nodded and smiled at adoring fans who clapped, whistled, and shouted, screaming his name. Many wore "I Saw Keefer Run" tee-shirts, others held up home-made signs painted in bright colors that said, "We love you Keefer."

Sandwiched between rollicking, echoing, cheers, the announcer recited highlights of Keefer's career. Winner, 42 races in 57 starts. Winner, Derby Lane Inaugural. Winner, All-Star Kennel Preview. Winner, King & Queen Stake. Winner, 1986 Distance Classic. Winner, 1987 Distance Classic. Winner, Flashy Sir Award. Winner, All-America Award. Winner, All-World Sprint Team Award. Winner, All-World Distance Team Award.

It was impossible to deliver any kind of speech because people kept up a steady rumble and shout fest, trying to catch Keefer's eye. Folks didn't really care about his record on the track as much as they cared about Keefer himself. The admirers believed he belonged to them, to everyone, and, indeed, the Greyhound behaved as if he did, doling out affection to one and all with egalitarian fervor. He was the people's Greyhound, the people's choice, the darling they adored and vowed never to forget. Indeed, 20 years later, people who had seen Keefer at Derby Lane remembered him with the clarity of a dearly beloved friend still present, still vibrantly alive in the mind and heart.

EPILOGUE

with love,
KEEFER

The Dillon-Schulthess partnership rattled to a halt soon after Keefer's retirement from racing life.

*Postcard showcasing Keefer winning
the Derby Lane Distance Classic, 1986.*

Epilogue

The Dillon-Schulthess partnership rattled to a halt soon after Keefer's retirement from racing life. O'Keeffe was the only journalist to present a detailed version of the story, which appeared in the *Tampa Tribune* under the headline, "Kennel Team Splits Up After Differences."

Keith Dillon and Jim Schulthess who combined to send more great Greyhounds to post at Derby Lane in the past 10 years than any other team, have dissolved their partnership.

Kennel owner Dillon confirmed the rumor last week from his Olathe, Kansas farm. "I guess you can just say {Schulthess} resigned," he said as he chose his words very slowly and carefully.

Schulthess, who was the kennel manager for 12 years with Dillon, said he didn't resign. "Keith asked me to resign, but I told him I had never quit anything, and I wasn't going to do it with this job."

Schulthess' last day working for Dillon was June 2. "I didn't like some of the things I was hearing near the end of the Derby Lane meet," Dillon said. "I just thought it was time for a change, and the dogs have really been running good up here {at Southland}."

Jerry Maddox, who assisted Schulthess, was promoted to the number one position. Maddox has worked the Tampa Bay circuit for a number of years and worked with Schulthess about two years.

Schulthess said the thing that cost him his job was Dillon finally believed all of the rumors he had been hearing. "I know the rumors had been wild. Everyone said I was on drugs, in a drug rehab center and everything else.

All I can say is that I went and took a drug test, signed a release for Keith to get the report and he never called to even get it.

I don't know where the drug stories started, but they've been around for some time now."

Schulthess admitted he drank more this year at Derby Lane than probably ever before. "Keith knew I liked to drink a little bit before he hired me, but it never bothered him."

He said most of the drinking at Derby Lane resulted from other problems he was having in his life. The biggest was that he and his wife, Jane, separated during the spring.

"I don't think Keith liked that I moved out. Some of the rumors he was hearing were true, but most of them weren't."

That was the last article O'Keeffe wrote about the Dillon-Schulthess partnership. There was nothing more to say. It was finished, just as his own 28-year tenure as a sports writer would be finished ten years later. Increasingly disillusioned with the corporate "squeeze every nickel and dime" direction he saw the newspaper environment heading, he accepted a position at St. Petersburg College in April of 1997.

In the fall of 2006, his title at the College was Assistant Director of Institutional Advancement. Although his job involved media, promotions and advertising, the 55-year-old was a long way from writing sports news. His visits to Greyhound racetracks were sparse, limited to big events such as the Derby Lane Million, launched in 2006.

The inaugural Derby Lane Million—"the richest Greyhound race in the world"— brought almost 10,000 people to the St. Petersburg track, the most it had seen since Keefer days. The boost in attendance was temporary. After the million dollar race, live numbers slumped back down again. It was just too easy for bettors to go to the corner bar or other off-track betting site to wager on races at tracks all over the country. Still, Derby Lane persevered, as always.

O'Keeffe recalled that Derby Lane's president, Art Weaver, told him in 1985 that making races available on television would take away the urgency to go out to the track. Of course, Art was right. But, knowing the problems ahead can be useful as a guide to avoid—or outsmart—the pitfalls. Certainly, Art Weaver's presidential leadership from 1980 to 2003 spanned some of the toughest years that Derby Lane—or any parimutuel racetrack—ever faced. Somehow, he—and his family—managed to stay a few steps ahead of the flame-throwing dragon that had a taste for devouring competition. About the time the Florida State Lottery emerged as a major force in the late 1980s, Art unfurled a fledgling concept called simulcast wagering that allowed bettors from all over the country to wager on Derby Lane's races. The innovation was a groundbreaking savior for his organization, as it would be for racetracks around the country—and the world. Not one to rest easy on laurels—or dawdle in the glories of the past—Art forged further into the safety zone by seeing Derby Lane become the first to offer its Greyhound races on the Internet. In 1999, he ventured into uncharted territory with the creation of the Greyhound Channel that evolved to include account wagering. In 2001, he and partners expanded the concept overseas with Euro Off-Track. He was first to introduce Irish racing simulcasts in America with the premiere of the Irish Greyhound Derby and weekly races on a limited basis. The various high tech advancements expanded wager pool possibilities, but didn't boost live attendance that had dwindled with the advent of the state-supported lottery and other local attractions. In a gesture reminiscent of his grandfather, Art welcomed other entertainment venues into Derby Lane, such as low-stakes poker, when Florida legislation passed in 1997 to allow such games at parimutuel sites. While Art never wavered from the family's mission to preserve Greyhound racing, he recognized the need to lure fresh faces and revenue onto the Gandy Boulevard property that loomed so large.

In June of 2003, after 23 years at the helm, Art shifted into the position of Chairman of the Board. He was 77, the same age T.L. had been when he vacated the presidency in 1947. Art's only son, Vey O. Weaver, moved into the presidential slot. Like previous changings of the guard, no ripple was apparent in the organization's operation. Vey's apprenticeship had been years in the making, with him working quietly alongside his father, listening, absorbing, learning, patiently anticipating the day it would be his turn to step into the leadership role. When Art died unexpectedly the day after Christmas of 2004, there was a sharp shudder in the passage, but the grand ship steamed on without pause exactly as four generations of Weavers intended. The power of the past fused with the gritty competitive present served as propelling fuel.

Beginning in November of 2006, Greyhound racing in West Memphis, Arkansas, was powered by a new fuel source. Approved by the voting public, "games of skill" clinked and whirred, challenging patrons to step up and play to win. While live attendance for Greyhound racing didn't substantially increase, purses paid to kennel operators nearly doubled thanks to shiny machines showcased in a 40 million-dollar renovation. The combination of gaming and racing assured Southland a firm foothold on a well-paved path into the future.

Kip Keefer probably wouldn't recognize the facility where his career, and an abiding passion, for Greyhound racing began. This Renaissance man carved a path into his future by immersing himself in a variety of racetrack positions that included announcer, general manager, industry consultant, publicist, track-opening specialist, and trainer. In 2004, he became Director of the Birmingham Racing Commission, a post he still held in the fall of 2006. Through it all, the outspoken aficionado found time to hone his broadcasting skills, helping to pioneer, then anchor the first 13 editions of Greyhound racing's Night Of Stars. He also hosted his own radio program featuring parimutuel sports.

The term "Renaissance man" was certainly coined to describe achievers like Keith Dillon. In addition to maintaining stellar kennel and breeding operations, he served as President of the Greyhound Hall of Fame for 16 years following his two-term presidency of the National Greyhound Association. Steering both organizations ably through controversy and turmoil, he could have rested on his accomplishments, retiring when Keefer retired from the track. Approaching his 72nd birthday in 1987, he was well past retirement age by most people's standards, but Dillon didn't follow the path most people took. He continued doing what he had always done on his farm—birth and raise Greyhounds, train them, send them off to the races. In the late 1980s, he began reducing the numbers he raised by about half from 30 to 15 or 20 Greyhounds a year. His racers always performed well at the track, though the Dillon-Schulthess high-water mark achieved during the 1980s was definitely a pinnacle.

While Dillon respected the past, he was not mired there. He accepted—indeed, embraced—change when change was essential. After parimutuel wagering was legalized in Kansas in 1989, Dillon engineered major change by moving his Greyhounds to the newly opened Woodlands racetrack in Kansas City. The track was much closer to his farm and had year-round racing dates. Instead of securing his own kennel contract at the Woodlands, he leased his Greyhounds to a kennel that already had a contract.

The time was right to make changes because Viv had health challenges that required Dillon's attention. The trademark determination he had always shown in the Greyhound racing world was put to the test in his personal life. When Viv fell and broke a hip that put her into a rehab hospital, complications from Diabetes and other illnesses compromised her recovery. Viv's doctor advised that she be moved to a nursing facility, but Dillon said no, he would take her home. The doubting doctor shook her head. "Now, Keith," she remarked, "There's no way you can take care of her." He looked the doctor square in the eye, and replied, "You just try me." With that, he bundled Viv up and they went home together where he tended her until she died in 2003.

As of fall, 2006, Dillon was still making the twice-a-year trip to Abilene, Kansas, for gatherings that included Greyhound races and auctions as well as ceremonies connected to the National Greyhound Association and Greyhound Hall of Fame.

That Dillon would still be going strong in his 91st year would be no surprise to those who knew him. During their long partnership, Jim Schulthess came to know the man as well as anyone except, perhaps, Dillon's wife. When the two men became partners in 1976, 51-year-old Dillon had over 35 years of success under his belt. The 29-year-old Schulthess was still wet behind the ears when it came to

Greyhound racing, but he was eager and willing to learn, much as Dillon had been when he started in his twenties. Together, the pair formed a complementary, and formidably effective, kennel. Dillon sent well-bred and well-prepared Greyhounds to Schulthess, who, in turn, managed racetrack careers, nurturing and, thus, enabling the racers to achieve their ultimate potential. Together, the combined force of Dillon and Schulthess sailed into Greyhound racing history.

History, of course, cannot stop time or prevent change. When Schulthess and Dillon split, the two men's paths diverged. Dillon hunkered down and continued in the sport he'd known for 49 years. Schulthess, in contrast, left Greyhound racing altogether. He told O'Keeffe he was uncertain where he would earn his next paycheck, but he thought he might "open up a bar or something." He indicated he had been contacted by more than one person interested in getting started in the [racing] business with him, but he didn't want any deal other than the one he'd had with Dillon, which was 50/50, an unusually lucrative arrangement at the time between a kennel owner/operator and a kennel manager.

What Schulthess did was buy a check-cashing business and liquor store in St. Petersburg in the months following the partnership break-up. While the business was successful, it didn't carry the challenge and thrill of Greyhound racing. There were no Greyhounds at all to keep the days and nights exciting. After about ten years, when he'd cashed enough checks and sold enough booze to last a lifetime, Schulthess put the businesses up for sale.

On the home front, sultry Xandra became a memory Schulthess preferred to forget, a symbol of how we can fool ourselves with vulnerable missteps. He and Jane reconciled soon after Keefer's last race and they remained married for a number of additional years. Eventually, though, the couple divorced.

After selling the businesses in Florida, Schulthess returned to Greyhound racing in the late 1990s, ending up as a hired trainer at Bluffs Run Casino and Greyhound Park in Council Bluffs, Iowa. While there, he developed a relationship with Linda Willey, who would become trainer for the Neal Blake Kennel. After training RA Blazer, the highest earning Greyhound ever (a racing income record that stood until the 2006 Derby Lane Million), Willey indicated in the January 2005 issue of The Greyhound Review that, "she learned the business from her fiancé Jim Schulthess." Given Willey's accomplishments with RA Blazer, the tribute to Schulthess carried particular heft.

One thing led to another and Schulthess found himself ruled off the racetrack in Council Bluffs. "I got into it with a state official," he remarked. "I stand my ground. When I'm right, I'm right. When I'm wrong, I still think I'm right." The punishment was a five-year license suspension. Schulthess appealed, but to no avail. Greyhound racing was out of his life again. In a way, the timing meshed with the sharp tines of time. Schulthess' aged mother in Haven, Kansas, wasn't doing very well, so he returned to his hometown to help with her care. Along the way, he underwent back surgery that compromised his ability to work. Even if he wanted to return to Greyhound racing, his condition—and the very physical work of a trainer's life—most likely wouldn't allow it. After his mother passed on in 2006, he remained in Haven, recuperating from surgery and contemplating his next move in the chess-game of life.

The chess-game of life can be slow and ponderous. It can also be full of surprises. Keefer settled comfortably into life on the Dillon farm with his new title, stud. He didn't exactly loll around all day. In fact, he still had the exuberance of a youthful, energetic, pup, and he often annoyed the grey-faced elders—his father, Perceive, Understood, Bold Footprint, and others.

Given his success on the racetrack and his stellar pedigree, Keefer's reproductive service was much in demand. The substantial $1,500 fee didn't deter parties willing to send their females to Dillon to be artificially inseminated with Keefer's semen. People were willing to spend even more than the asking price. At a National Greyhound Association auction, stud service to Keefer brought a record $2,500. Keefer's racing income of $128,000 plus his $313,000 breeding fees pushed his total career earnings to $440,000, an impressive figure in any era.

The website, Greyhound-Data.com, reflects that Keefer produced over 500 offspring. The surprise was not the number, but that no superstars flowed from Keefer's superstar genes. Looking back, Dillon lamented this fact. He expressed surprise at how it could possibly be true, and recited some of Keefer's stand-out lineage. "His father (Perceive) was a 3-time All-American, his mother (Position) was an All-American, his grandmother (Abella) was an All-American. His grandfather (Downing) was an All American."

Keefer should have produced winners that were equal or better than he was, but he didn't. There might have been a hint of what was to come in the Perceive-Position litter that produced Keefer. Of the five pups, he was the only one to shine on the track. His sister, Fun Size, was successful, but only if she had the lead. For that, Schulthess called her, "phony as an $8 bill." In contrast, Keefer's father, Perceive, hailed from a quality litter of Greyhounds that proved their mettle on the track. Schulthess said he wished he had the others to train, but Perceive was the only pup Dillon got out of the Downing-Lucky Carmell litter, a lucky pick because Perceive was, by far, the most impressive. Keefer's mother, Position, also hailed from a litter of able racers. In addition to Position's accomplishments, her sisters, Visible and Preview, exhibited memorable talent on the track, as well. Whatever the cause—biology, fate, luck—Keefer was a freak in his litter—a freak of talent, determination, size, charisma.

Had Keefer been as successful in the breeding arena as he was on the racing oval, he would undoubtedly have joined his father and grandfather in the Greyhound Hall of Fame. As the chess-game played out, Keefer was not to be memorialized in the hallowed hall. Instead, he would be remembered with fond affection by the many people whose lives he touched—Dillon and Schulthess, to be sure, and certainly his legion of fans who would never have been content to watch him on a television screen or a laptop computer. He was a big strapping Greyhound that people wanted to experience in-the-flesh, a Greyhound whose charismatic presence spoke volumes in a visceral way. Keefer's lasting mark, then, could never be fully captured on a plaque, a screen, or in a book. Rather, his mark was the more tangible sort that brought people to the track, the paddock, the kennel, the farm—wherever he was, they wanted to be, engaging all the senses, feeling what they could not adequately describe, but could never forget.

Pedigree

		Big Whizzer	Westy Whizzer	Tell You Why *
		RBD, 1970		Kinto Nebo
	Downing		Tulia	Julius Caesar *
	RBD, 1975			Calesa
		Hooker's Flower	My Friend Lou	Ample Tip
		RF, 1967		Win Dixie
Perceive			Good M.	Johnny M.
RBD, 1979				Comply
		SS. Jeno	Venerated	Ample Time
		BD, 1970		Viewed *
	Lucky Carmell		Kitty Hoss	Metal Jet *
	WF, 1976			Kathi Award
		Lucky Terra	Lucky Bannon	Michigan Jack
		R, 1971		Valoretta
			Pree	New World
				Shop Talk
KEEFER				
Red, 1984				
		Newdown Heather	Printer's Prince	Hi There
		WBK, 1964		Sally's Gossip
				The Grand
	Dillard *		Pardee	Champion
	BK, 1971			Manhattan Heiress
		Orwell Parade	Racing Rory	Knock Hill Chieftain
		BD, 1966		Burleigh's Fancy
			Orwell Wonder	Pigalle Wonder
Position				Top Level
FBD, 1978		Lucky Bannon	Michigan Jack	Julius Caesar *
		R, 1967		My Lucky Gertie
	Abella		Valoretta	Great Valor
	RBD, 1972			Lahoma Judy
		Orange Ice	Lios Mire *	Knock Hill Chieftain
		DKF, 1966		Lady Lou.
			Bouncy Belle	Cleveland Lad *
				Lady's Miss

Adapted from Greyhound-Data.com

Acknowledgements

*K*eefer: The People's Choice is a work of creative nonfiction. The scenes portrayed sprang from my imagination based on my interpretation of thoughts and experiences conveyed to me in interviews. Facts related to Keefer's racing career flowed from newspaper clips and magazine articles, with supplementation from extensive personal interviews I conducted. Names are real with the exception of Lou and Xandra. Versions of Chapters One and Six were published in *The Greyhound Review*.

Writing about a racing Greyhound of the past is a challenge made doubly difficult because there are so few books written about the sport. In fact, Paul C. Hartwell's, *The Road From Emeryville* is the only book devoted to the history of American Greyhound racing, and it leaves off at 1980! Many fine articles and profiles have been written through the years, but the articles are scattered throughout publications such as *The Greyhound Review, Turn-Out, Greyhound Racing Record, Greyhound Update.* Only *The Greyhound Review* remains active. When the other venues shut down, entire collections disappeared from easy access. These days, the only way to obtain vintage issues is to get lucky on Ebay, meet an old-timer who has stashed the material somewhere, or visit the archives of the National Greyhound Hall of Fame with its eclectic assortment of donated historical goods. To be sure, the process is hit-or-miss.

When documentation is scattered or scarce, people become the vital link, and that was true in the preparation of this book. In fact, without the many people who offered time and attention, the book could not have been completed.

First and foremost, I wish to extend thanks to Keith Dillon who welcomed Keefer into the world and owned the champion throughout his life. Mr. Dillon supported this project from the moment I mentioned that I would like to take it on. Not only did he devote much of his own time to talk with me, but he offered access to his tremendous scrapbook and memorabilia. He also helped me locate Jim Schulthess, his long-time partner and trainer of Keefer. Over several months in the fall of 2006 and spring of 2007, Mr. Schulthess graciously spent hours upon hours sharing his recollections. Fortunately, we both had flat-rate long-distance plans on our telephones. Early on, he loaned me a big box of one-of-a-kind items related to Keefer and other champions that raced for the Dillon/Schulthess kennel between 1976 and 1987. Filled with photographs, award mementos, hand-written notes, purse sheets, old programs, and yellowed newspaper clippings, the musty material told its own kind of story.

The list of people who shared memories and memorabilia about Keefer is long. I found some of the folks on my own, but many were referrals. To the following individuals, I owe deepest appreciation and earnest thanks:

Kip Keefer, of Birmingham, Alabama, whose unflagging commitment to Greyhound racing can be traced to the Dillon/Schulthess superstars that wowed him at Southland and Derby Lane in the 1980s;

Mike O'Keeffe, of St. Petersburg, Florida, who dug deep as a sports reporter during Keefer's reign to write impressive weekly columns about Greyhound racing;

Gail Hesse and Dr. Lester McLachlan of St. Petersburg, Florida, who bought their first Greyhound from Keith Dillon many years ago and have been enjoying Greyhounds at the track and in their home ever since;

Lewinda "Windy" Roban of Ft. White, Florida, who grew up with Greyhounds on her grandmother, Dorothy Roban's, farm. Windy's favorite Greyhound of all time was "White Ruffles," a daughter of Keefer's;

Bill Bell, who has worked at Derby Lane for 36 years in a variety of positions ranging from leadout to judge, racing secretary, and plant supertintendent;

Don Cuddy, of Ireland, often referred to as the best of the best trainers of racing Greyhounds;

Myra and Jesse Sullivan of West Memphis, Arkansas, a husband and wife team who have worked at Southland since it opened its doors in 1956. Myra, in fact, started working there the year before it opened. Between them, they have over a 100 years of experience and knowledge of Southland Greyhound Park. To say they are loyal supporters is an understatement.

Very special thanks go to Louise Weaver, Assistant Vice President and Historian of Derby Lane, who embraced the project with vast enthusiasm and extreme diligence. Not only did she send me thick envelopes of well-documented newspaper clippings, articles, and vintage photographs related to Keefer's career at her family's venerable track, but she wrote a detailed history of Derby Lane to aid my research and writing. Her meticulous attention to detail deserves a gold medal. Thanks as well to Gary Guccione and Paul Hartwell for ever-ready answers and anecdotes.

To my husband, Jerry Baldwin, I offer heartfelt thanks for giving me the gift of time to complete the book, and for patiently listening to my fusillade of endless talk about a Greyhound he'd never heard of, but came to know well as the project progressed.

Finally, to Keefer, I extend thanks and a note: your ability to bring people together lives on. Viva Keefer.

Bibliography

During my research, I had access to newspaper clippings, magazine articles, photos, and other memorabilia related to Keefer. Frequently, the material did not contain complete reference identification. In such cases, I have inserted "SB" for unknown publication or incomplete citation and/or "n.d." for no date available.

"28th Annual Distance Classic, Tenth Race." Derby Lane Program. 21 February 1987.

"1980-1989." National Geographic Eyewitness to the 20th Century. Washington DC: National Geographic Society, 1998. 315-345.

Baal, Steve. "Can Keefer Set Derby Lane Record?" St. Petersburg Evening Independent. 4 April 1986.

—-. "Derby Lane Fans Have Bad Case of Keefer Fever." St. Petersburg Evening Independent. SB, (after) 22 Feb 1986.

—-. "Keefer Comes Back, But Can Only Show." St. Petersburg Times. n.d.

—-. "Keefer's Championship Season." National Greyhound Update. SB 1986. 41-46.

—-. "Keefer's Healthy and He's Back at Derby Lane." St. Petersburg Times. 17 Jan 1987.

—-. "Exit His 'I Saw Keefer Run' T-shirt." Greyhound Update. SB (after) 8 April 1987.

Bell, William "Bill." Telephone interview. 16 Nov 2006.

Black, Jay. "Keefer ... A True Champion." SB (approx) 10 April 1987.

—-. "Late Charging Keefer Triumphs in St. Pete Inaugural." SB 1986.

Chick, Bob. "They Wanted a Lawyer." SB, n.d.

Cuddy, Don. Telephone interview. 24 Nov 2006.

"Derby Lane." St. Petersburg Evening Independent. 7 May 1986.

"Derby Lane's New King." SB, n.d.

"Derby Lane Standout Keefer Ready to Resume Racing Career." St. Petersburg Times. 1August 1986.

Dillon, Keith. Telephone interview. 14 Oct 2005, 12 & 20 Oct 2006, 21 Feb 2007.

Farley, Greg. "Cuddy's Over-the-Hill Gang Wow's 'Em at Wonderful." The Greyhound Review. Aug 1976. 92-93.

Filipelli, Vera. "Derby Lane Turns 80." The Greyhound Review. Jan 2005. 41-44.

—-. "Obituary of Art Weaver." The Greyhound Review. Feb 2005. 5.

Fry, Darrell. "Just Listen: all the talk's about Keefer." Tampa Tribune. SB (after) 22 Feb 1986.

—-. "Keefer Will Miss Derby, Rest of Race Season With Injury." St. Petersburg Times. 3 May 1986. 8C.

"Greyhound Industry Mourns Passing of John Brooks, 68." Greyhound Racing Record. 2 May 1959. 2.

Guccione, Gary. "Dream Weaver." The Greyhound Review. Feb 2005. 3.

—-. Great Names in Greyhound Pedigrees, Vol. II, The Eighties. Topeka, KS: Hall Directory, Inc., 1993.

—-. "His Very Best Shot." The Greyhound Review. Dec 1983. 32-39.

—-. "Traffic Officer (April 1925)." Greyhound Breeder's Journal. Topeka, KS: Hall Directory, Inc., 1977. 141-2.

Hartwell, Paul C. Email to author. 23 Jan 2007.

—-. The Road to Emeryville: A History of Greyhound Racing. California Research Publishing, 1980.

Hesse, Gail & Dr. Lester McLachlan. Telephone interview. 18 Nov 2006.

Hines, Nathaniel D. "Leg Injury Puts a Cramp in Keefer's Racing Schedule." St. Petersburg Times. 13 April 1987.

Horan, Tim. "Blazin a Trail in Iowa." The Greyhound Review. Jan 2005. 75-6

—-. "Dillon's Specialty is All-Americans, 'miracle litters'." Greyhound Racing Record. Aug 1984. 6-9.

"Keefer Breaks All-Time Win Records at Derby Lane." Greyhound Charts. 3 May 1986.

"Keefer Drops Out of Wonderland Derby." SB, 25 Aug 1986.

"Keefer Four-For-Four With All-Star Win." SB, n.d.

Keefer, Kip. "Havencroft: Carrying on a Winning Tradition." The Greyhound Racing Record. 26 Nov 1983. 16-17.

—-. "Keefer on Keefer." National Greyhound Update. SB, n.d. 33-38.

—-. "Perceive: Thanks for the Memories." Greyhound Racing Record. 15 Oct 1983. 20-23.

—-. "Remembering Understood ... What Might Have Been." Unpublished article. 1983.

—-. Telephone interview. 29 Oct 2006.

—-. "The Greatest Sprinter in Greyhound Racing History? A Case for Perceive." Greyhound Racing Record. 9 July 1983. 20-23.

—-. "The Man at the Track." Turnout. July 1985. 31.

"Keefer Prepares for Wonderland Derby." SB, 16 Aug 1986.

"Keefer Repeats as Distance Classic Champ." Weekly Greyhound Charts. 7 March 1987. 1.

"Keefer Sweeps Distance Classic Qualifying Rounds." SB, n.d.

"Keefer's Season Ends in Pain." St. Petersburg Times. 10 April 1987. Front Page, Sports Section.

Kulchinsky, Aaron. Nomination of Joyce Weaver Brooks to Greyhound Hall of Fame. n.d.

Moshier, Jeff. "Derby Lane Completes Major Expansion." Greyhound Racing Record. 12 Dec 1970. 3.

O'Keeffe, Mike. "Growth Slowdown Reaches Derby Lane." Tampa Tribune. 5 May 1986. 10-C.

—. "Keefer Is Getting Ready to Get Back on Track." Tampa Tribune. 24 Nov 1986.

—. "Keefer Out Tonight With Leg Injury." Tampa Tribune. 26 April 1986. 8-C.

—. "Keefer Returns Wednesday, and He's As Good As Ever." Tampa Tribune. 19 Jan 1987.

—. "Keefer's Legacy." Greyhound USA. June 1986. 15.

—. "Keefer's Lightning-Fast Start Made Classic a 1-dog Race." Tampa Tribune. SB (after) 22 Feb 1986.

—. "Keefer's Recuperation Period Continues Down Along the Mississippi." Tampa Tribune. 2 June 1986.

—. "Keefer's Reincarnation." Greyhound USA. Jan 1987.

—. "Kennel Team Splits Up After Differences." Tampa Tribune. SB (approx) 4 July 1987. 8-C.

—. "Leg Injury will Keep Keefer Out of Derby." Tampa Tribune. 3 May 1986.

—. "Odds Against Keefer's Return." Tampa Tribune. 22 Sept 1986. 12-C.

—. "Pulled Muscle May End Keefer's Racing Career." Tampa Tribune. 10 April 1987. Front Page, Sports Section.

—. Telephone interview. 7 Nov 2006.

Parent, Joseph. Mastering the Mental Game. www.zen-golf.com. 23 Jan 2007.

Roban, Lewinda "Windy." Telephone interview. 10 Nov 2006.

Samuels, David. "Going to the Dogs." Harper's Magazine. Feb 1999. 52-63.

Schulthess, Jim. Telephone interview. 20 Oct 2006; 10, 18, & 30 Nov 2006; 18 & 27 Dec 2006; 17 Jan 2007; 21 & 24 Feb 2007.

Schwadel, Francine. "Red-Hot Racing Dog Wins People's Hearts Even When He Fails." Wall Street Journal. 16 April 1986.

Sullivan, Jesse & Myra. Telephone interview. 24 Jan 2007.

"T.L. "Dad" Weaver Dies." Greyhound Racing Record. 4 April 1952. 4.

"Traffic Officer." American Greyhound Racing Encyclopedia. American Greyhound Track Operators Association, 1963. 108-9.

"The Winning Alternative: Artificial Lure Training." Video produced by the American Greyhound Track Operators Association and the National Greyhound Association in cooperation with Hill & Knowlton, Inc. 1976.

Weaver, Louise. "Derby Lane History." Unpublished document. 27 Jan 2007.

Wootten, Leslie. "Profile of Keith Dillon." Part 1 of 3.

The Greyhound Review. March 2006. 33-35.

—-. "Profile of Keith Dillon." Part 2 of 3. The Greyhound Review. April 2006. 33-36.

—-. "Profile of Keith Dillon." Part 3 of 3. The Greyhound Review. May 2006. 48-51.

Photo Credits

Front Cover. Keefer wins Derby Lane Distance Classic, 1987 (courtesy, Maddock Photography).

Chapter 1 (a). Keith Dillon and My Judy, winner's circle, Tampa, 1941 (courtesy, Keith Dillon).

Chapter 1 (b). Keith Dillon and the "miracle litter," 1950s (courtesy, Keith Dillon).

Chapter 2 (a). Jim Schulthess (right), winner's circle, Tucson Greyhound Park, 1972 (courtesy, Jim Schulthess).

Chapter 2 (b). Jim Schulthess and Perceive, 1981 All American (courtesy, Jim Schulthess).

Chapter 3. Perceive's retirement ceremony at Southland Greyhound Park, 1983. Jim Schulthess (behind Perceive) is flanked by Keith and Vivian Dillon (courtesy, Kip Keefer).

Chapter 4. Derby Lane, 1925 (courtesy, Tampa-Hillsborough County Public Library System).

Chapter 5. Jim Schulthess and Havencroft, 1982 (courtesy, Jim Schulthess).

Chapter 6. Traffic Officer (courtesy, National Greyhound Association).

Chapter 7. Keefer in meditative mode, up-close (courtesy, Kip Keefer).

Chapter 8. A view of Keefer's body, au naturel, 1986 (courtesy, Kip Keefer).

Chapter 9. Keefer wins Derby Lane Inaugural, 1986 (courtesy, Maddock Photography).

Chapter 10. Keefer and Keefer, 1986 (courtesy, Kip Keefer).

Chapter 11. Record crowd at Derby Lane for Keefer's Distance Classic win, 1986 (courtesy, Maddock Photography).

Chapter 12. Jim Schulthess, Keith Dillon and Keefer accepting the trophy for Derby Lane's Distance Classic, 1986 (courtesy, Maddock Photography).

Chapter 13. Keefer makes tracks north, 1986 (from National Greyhound Update Magazine).

Chapter 14. Keefer at Dillon's Olathe farm (courtesy, Gail Hesse).

Chapter 15. Keefer wins Derby Lane Distance Classic, 1987 (courtesy, Maddock Photography).

Chapter 16. Up-close view of Keefer smiling, 1986 (courtesy, Maddock Photography).

Chapter 17. Keefer wins Derby Lane All Star Kennel Preview, 1986 (courtesy, Maddock Photography).

Epilogue. Postcard showcasing Keefer winning the Derby Lane Distance Classic, 1986 (photo courtesy, Maddock Photography; postcard courtesy, Derby Lane).

Back Cover. A view of Keefer's body, au naturel, 1986 (courtesy, Kip Keefer). Leslie A. Wootten with pet Greyhounds, Annie and Louise, 2006 (courtesy, the author).